# A Man's Workbook

# Other Publications by Stephanie S. Covington

## Spanish Books

*La mujer y su práctica de los Doce Pasos (A Woman's Way through the Twelve Steps)*

*La mujer y su práctica de los Doce Pasos: Libro de ejercicios (A Woman's Way through the Twelve Steps Workbook)*

*Mujeres en recuperación: Entendiendo la adicción (Women in Recovery: Understanding Addiction)*

*Voces: Un programa de autodescubrimiento y empoderamiento para chicas guía del facilitador (Voices: A Program of Self-Discovery and Empowerment for Girls facilitator guide)*

*Voces: Un programa de autodescubrimiento y empoderamiento para chicas diario (Voices: A Program of Self-Discovery and Empowerment for Girls journal)*

## Other Publications by Dan Griffin

*A Man's Way Through the Twelve Steps*

*A Man's Way through Relationships: Learning to Love and Be Loved*

*Amazing Dads!*

*Amazing Dads!* (curriculum), with Harrison Crawford

*Healing Men's Pain*, with Jonathan DeCarlo

Second Edition

HELPING MEN RECOVER

# A Man's Workbook

A PROGRAM FOR TREATING ADDICTION

Stephanie S. Covington, Dan Griffin,
and Rick Dauer

**JB JOSSEY-BASS™**
A Wiley Brand

*Registered Office*

John Wiley & Sons, Inc., 111 River Street, Hoboken, NJ 07030, USA

*Editorial Office*

111 River Street, Hoboken, NJ 07030, USA

For details of our global editorial offices, customer services, and more information about Wiley products visit us at www.wiley.com.

Wiley also publishes its books in a variety of electronic formats and by print-on-demand. Some content that appears in standard print versions of this book may not be available in other formats.

*Library of Congress Cataloging-in-Publication Data*

Names: Covington, Stephanie, author. | Griffin, Dan, 1972- author. | Dauer, Rick, author.
Title: Helping men recover : a program for treating addiction, a man's workbook/Stephanie S. Covington, Dan Griffin, and Rick Dauer.
Description: Second edition. | San Francisco : Jossey-Bass, 2022.
Identifiers: LCCN 2022025049 (print) | LCCN 2022025050 (ebook) | ISBN 9781119886556 (set) | ISBN 9781119886532 (paperback) | ISBN 9781119886563 (adobe pdf) | ISBN 9781119886495 (epub)
Subjects: LCSH: Male prisoners—Substance use. | Compulsive behavior—Treatment. | Substance abuse—Treatment. | Addicts—Rehabilitation.
Classification: LCC HV8836.5 .C674 2022 (print) | LCC HV8836.5 (ebook) | DDC 365/.667290811—dc23/eng/20220609
LC record available at https://lccn.loc.gov/2022025049
LC ebook record available at https://lccn.loc.gov/2022025050

Cover Design: Wiley
Cover Image: © Jasmin Merdan/Getty Images

Set in 11/16 pt Palatino LT Std by Straive, Chennai, India

SKY10047889_051623

# CONTENTS

# ABOUT THE AUTHORS

**Stephanie S. Covington**, PhD, LCSW, is an internationally recognized clinician, organizational consultant, and lecturer. For more than thirty years, her work has focused on the creation of gender-responsive and trauma-informed services. Her extensive experience includes designing women's services at the Betty Ford Center, developing programs for criminal justice settings, and being the featured therapist on the Oprah Winfrey Network TV show *Breaking Down the Bars*. She also has served as a consultant to the United Nations Office on Drugs and Crime in Vienna and was selected for the U.S. Advisory Committee for Women's Services. Educated at Columbia University and the Union Institute, Dr. Covington has conducted seminars for behavioral health professionals, community organizations, criminal justice professionals, and recovery groups in the United States, Canada, Mexico, Europe, Africa, Iceland, Brazil, the United Kingdom, and New Zealand. She has served on the faculties of the University of Southern California, San Diego State University, and the California School of Professional Psychology. She also has published extensively, including ten gender-responsive, trauma-informed treatment curricula. Dr. Covington is based in La Jolla, California, where she is co-director of the Institute for Relational Development and the Center for Gender and Justice.

**Dan Griffin**, MA, has worked in the addictions and mental health fields for more than twenty-five years, in research, case management, public advocacy, teaching, counseling, and drug courts. He is the author of *A Man's Way through the Twelve Steps* (2009), the first gender-responsive book for recovery for men; *A Man's Way through Relationships* (2014), the first trauma-informed and gender-responsive book to help men navigate the challenges of relationships and male socialization; and *Amazing Dads* (2022), the first trauma-informed book and curriculum (with Harrison Crawford) for fathers. Dan's graduate work focused on the transformation of masculinity in the Twelve Step culture. He is an international speaker and consultant who lives in LA with his wife and daughter. He has been in recovery since 1994.

**Rick Dauer**, LADC, is a behavioral health consultant and trainer. He has been a professional in the field of addiction since 1984 and has experience in residential, outpatient, and corrections-based treatment programs, including over twenty-five years as a clinical director. He has served on numerous state and national boards, panels, and task forces dedicated to improving access to high-quality substance use disorder services. He has long been an advocate for and practitioner of gender-responsive and trauma-informed care and he supervised the first pilot programs for both the *Helping Women Recover* and *Helping Men Recover* curricula. Rick lives in Saint Paul, Minnesota, and has been in recovery for over forty years.

# INTRODUCTION TO
## *HELPING MEN RECOVER*

# About This Program

*Helping Men Recover* addresses issues that many men struggle with, especially if they are experiencing problems with alcohol or other drugs. In most cases, you will be using this workbook as part of a program in which you meet regularly with a group of other recovering individuals. You will attend twenty-one sessions with them; together, you will develop new skills and new ways of thinking about yourselves. Your group will be led by a facilitator who has experience with addiction services and the process of recovery. He will offer you insights about the thoughts and feelings that you may experience as you do the work suggested in the sessions and in this workbook.

Although this workbook is designed for use in the *Helping Men Recover* program, you may use it by yourself or perhaps with the help of an addictions counselor or other helping professional. There are guidelines included for doing this.

The program is organized into four sections, or modules: Self, Relationships, Sexuality, and Spirituality. These are four areas that men consistently identify as the triggers for relapse and the areas of greatest change in their recoveries. Each person's process of recovery is unique, but most of us find that it involves discovering our true selves, connecting in healthy relationships with others, understanding our sexuality, and gaining some spiritual connection.

Within the four modules, specific topics are covered, including

- Self-awareness and identity
- How men are socialized in our society
- The impact of the family of origin
- Grounding and relaxation techniques
- Communication
- Power, violence, and abuse

- Relationships
- Trauma and addiction
- Sexual identity
- Healthy sexuality
- What spirituality is

Awareness is the first step toward change. When you become aware of your addiction, you can decide to begin a process of recovery. When you become more aware of yourself and your relationships, you can make changes in your life. So the journey is about discovery as well as recovery. As you begin to think, feel, and act differently, you begin to heal and to connect with and value all parts of yourself—inner as well as outer.

# Program Goals

The goals of the *Helping Men Recover* program are

- To provide a safe place to reflect and learn more about yourself
- To learn about men, addiction, and trauma
- To develop the skills necessary for developing healthy and growth-fostering relationships
- To learn skills for maintaining recovery
- To identify the life you want to live

# This Revised Edition

*Helping Men Recover* originally was designed as a gender-based, trauma-informed treatment program for men with substance-use disorders. Over the years, our understanding of gender has shifted from the binary male-female model to a more inclusive and expansive model. We now know that sexual identity and gender identity can be more fluid; each exists across a continuum. Therefore, one of the revisions to this program is to make it suitable for men, trans men, and nonbinary people who have a masculine experience of the world. Other revisions include the updating of research, theories, practices, and contents of the sessions.

# INTRODUCTION TO
# *A MAN'S WORKBOOK*

This workbook is a tool to help you with your growth and recovery. You will be using it alone or as part of a *Helping Men Recover* program. It is a place to record your experiences, thoughts, feelings, and what you learn during the group sessions and for activities that you will be doing on your own between the sessions. This workbook contains

- A brief summary of the material covered during each session
- Questions that may be used during the subgroup discussions
- Space in which to complete activities during the group sessions
- Copies of charts and illustrations discussed in the group sessions
- Additional information, references, and resources related to the topics of the sessions
- Questions and activities to encourage further reflection outside the group
- Specific assignments to be completed by the next session
- Space to reflect on how the session material relates to your recovery

The activities that are to be completed between the group sessions are designed to help you to reflect on what you have learned, to practice some new skills and behaviors, and to consider the benefits of what you are practicing. Some of them involve writing or drawing, but your skills in these areas are not being tested. You do not need to worry about your handwriting or spelling. There are no right or wrong answers, and your work will not be checked or graded. Your workbook is for your use only. No one will judge what you say. No one else will read any of it without your permission. What matters is what you put into the activities and, consequently, what you get out of them.

If there is any writing to be done, there are spaces provided for that. If you have a hard time writing what you want to say, it's okay to draw pictures or use abbreviations instead. It's also okay to work on these activities with another group member and to help each other. Asking for help can be tough for some people.

Your recovery will depend, in part, on your willingness to ask for help, so this would be a good place to begin.

When you begin to use this workbook after a group session or on your own, take a minute or two to unwind, relax, and focus on where you are now. Just get settled in the way that feels best for you. Allow yourself to notice how you're breathing and then inhale gently and exhale fully. Repeat the breathing exercise two more times.

You may be concerned about keeping your workbook private. If you live with others and are not sure that they will respect your privacy, you should hide your workbook or lock it up. Or you can ask the facilitator or another counselor to help you find ways to keep your workbook safe between group sessions. The facilitator(s) are prepared for such requests. If the facilitator will be holding your workbook between the sessions, he will respect your privacy and will arrange for you to complete the extra activities after each session or at some other time.

It is important that you bring your workbooks to each group session, so please try to remember that each time.

# Opening Session:
# Introduction to the Program

Your facilitator's name is _____.

Your co-facilitator's name (if there is one) is _____.

Your group will meet _____.

## Becoming Grounded

Being "grounded" means being able to remain present in the "here and now," even when experiencing powerful feelings. This session contains a couple of simple techniques that you can use by yourself when you are feeling uncomfortable or anxious or stressed. It is common and normal to occasionally feel uncomfortable, particularly when in a new group or when doing something unfamiliar.

Turn your attention inward and check out what is going on in your body. You may close your eyes or just lower your eyelids or focus by staring at something. Turn your attention to what you notice about yourself. Just curiously notice what you are feeling in your emotions and your body. Notice any areas of pain or tension or other sensations. Make any adjustments you need to help yourself feel more comfortable. See if anything changes as a result of your paying kind attention to it. You might notice your breath. Just allow yourself to explore your "felt" self for a bit.

*A Man's Workbook: Helping Men Recover, A Program for Treating Addiction,* Second Edition.
Stephanie S. Covington, Dan Griffin, and Rick Dauer.
© 2022 Stephanie S. Covington, Dan Griffin, and Rick Dauer. Published 2022 by John Wiley & Sons, Inc.

This is a settling and grounding activity. It helps you to be a bit more comfortable with where you are and what is going on inside you. For people who have struggled with addiction and for those who have experienced trauma, this is a very important skill to learn.

# Group Introductions

This group is a place for you to present yourself as you really are and to explore who you hope to become. It is a place to be your genuine self while supporting others who are doing the same thing. This program is created for men, trans men, and nonbinary people who have a masculine experience of the world. So, in order to be as inclusive as possible, we invite you to share your pronouns when you introduce yourselves.

If you are using this workbook on your own, read the questions and think about how you would introduce yourself to others.

1. My name:

   _____

2. When and where I was born:

   _____

   _____

3. How I identify myself (including culture, ethnicity, race, and pronouns):

   _____

   _____

4. The people in my family (can include a wife/husband or live-in partner, children, mother, father, brothers, sisters, or whomever you consider your immediate family):

   _____

   _____

   _____

5. One thing I like about myself or a special gift that I have:

   _____

   _____

# Goals of This Session

The goals of this session are

- To learn about the goals and structure of the program
- To begin to get to know one another and develop trust
- To create a list of group agreements
- To learn about men, addiction, and trauma
- To learn some relaxation and grounding activities

# Typical Session Contents

- Each session will begin with a time to settle in and prepare to do what you need to do during the group session. Group members will then check in with one another.
- Next, your group will discuss the Between-Sessions Activities from the previous session and talk briefly about the goals of the current session.
- In each session, there will be information presented on specific topics, followed by activities and discussions based on the information. There will be questions to help guide the group discussions.
- In each module, you will practice some relaxation and grounding activities.
- Because some of the content in these sessions may be difficult for you to think about and talk about, the facilitator will strive to make the group a safe and supportive place where you can experience your feelings and learn from them and also practice supporting the other members of the group. These techniques also may help you as you go through the process of learning to cope without using alcohol and other drugs.
- Toward the end of each session, you will hear about new Between-Sessions Activities that will provide the opportunity to put into practice the new concepts and skills you are learning.
- There also is a grounding activity at the end of each session.
- At the beginning and end of each module, there is a Recovery Scale. The purpose of this scale is for you to evaluate your own progress as you move through the program. No one else will see this.

# Program Sessions

Opening Session 1: Introduction to the Program

Module A: Self

     Session 2. Defining Self

     Session 3. Men in Recovery

     Session 4. A Sense of Self

     Session 5. Men, Inside and Out

     Session 6. Men and Feelings

Module B: Relationships

     Session 7. Family of Origin

     Session 8. Barriers to Healthy Relationships

     Session 9. Fathers

     Session 10. Mothers

     Session 11. Creating Healthy Relationships and Support Systems

     Session 12. Effective Communication

     Session 13. Creating and Maintaining Intimacy

Module C: Sexuality

     Session 14. Sexuality and Addiction

     Session 15. Sexual Identity

     Session 16. Barriers to Sexual Health

     Session 17. Healthy Sexuality

Module D: Spirituality

     Session 18. What Is Spirituality?

     Session 19. Power and Privilege

     Session 20. Building Resilience

     Session 21. Creating a Vision

# Examples of Group Agreements

If you are using this workbook individually, you may want to have some agreements with yourself (amount of time each day or week, etc.) while working through this program (see pages 6 and 7).

     If you are using this workbook in a group, you may want to place a check mark next to the agreements that your group adopts.

1. *Attendance*. We're all committing to show up at all the sessions. Your commitment to attend regularly helps to stabilize the group and creates an environment of mutual support. If you must miss a group session, please let a facilitator know in advance of that session. If you end up missing too many sessions, it may affect your ability to stay in the group. We also ask that you make a commitment to being on time for each session. A good way to do that is to try to be here five minutes before the session is supposed to start. If you are running late, please be sure to contact your facilitator.

2. *Confidentiality*. No personal information revealed in the group is to be repeated outside the room. There can be no trust if information about a group member is given to outsiders or if group members gossip about one another. There are two exceptions to this rule of confidentiality: (1) The facilitators have to communicate with other members of your treatment teams as part of your ongoing care; and (2) We are required by law to report to appropriate authorities when a member's personal safety or the safety of another person is at stake. You, as group members, will be responsible for maintaining confidentiality among yourselves.

3. *Safety*. It is important that each participant feels safe in the group. Safety includes feeling emotionally safe—feeling grounded and comfortable when sharing your thoughts and your problems with others. Our commitment is to make sure this is a safe group. In order for this to happen, we all need to agree that there will be no verbal, emotional, or physical abuse here.

4. *Engagement*. Everyone is invited to join in the discussions. We would all like to hear what you have to say. However, you always have the option to "pass." Please share all your remarks with the whole group. Your comments, questions, and opinions are of interest to all of us, and side remarks from one individual to another tend to distract and divide the group. Also, please keep the focus on the process of recovery. If you think that the group is getting off the topic, please feel free to mention this.

5. *Self-disclosure*. This is a program that invites you to share about yourself and your experiences. We want you to share only that with which you are comfortable. But we also want to encourage you to take risks and share information and parts of yourself that may feel vulnerable. Your vulnerability is your strength. It will be more helpful if you talk about your personal experiences, rather than about people in general, so speak with "I" statements rather than saying "they" or "you" or "we."

6. *Feedback*. The group members learn from one another. One of the ways this is done is by giving and getting feedback. If you do not want feedback, simply let

us know. If you are going to give feedback, please ask for permission first. Sometimes someone just wants to be heard. Always think about your motives for sharing feedback and make sure it is always for the benefit of the other person.

7. *Honesty*. We're here to tell the truth. Nobody will pressure you to tell anything about yourself that you don't want to talk about, but when you do talk, tell the truth about where you've been and how you feel.

8. *Respect*. When you tell the truth about what you think, please do so in a way that respects others in the group. That means no criticizing, judging, or talking down to anyone. If you think that someone is showing disrespect to someone else, please say so respectfully. If someone is dominating the conversation, the facilitator will referee so that everyone gets a chance to talk. If you feel uncomfortable or angry at some point and do not want to participate, do not disrupt the group. You can choose to be quiet until you feel more comfortable and are ready to participate again.

9. *Questions*. There are no bad questions or wrong answers, as long as you speak about what is true for you. Ask whatever is on your mind. Please respect one another's honest questions and opinions.

10. *Commitment to recovery*. It is important to be abstinent (or sober) when you come to each session. If you come while under the influence of alcohol or another drug, you will be asked to leave that day, and your status in the program will be evaluated. If you use mood-altering chemicals between treatment sessions, it is essential that you inform your facilitator or another staff person as soon as possible.

# My Group's Agreements

Are there any additional agreements that your group adopted that are not on the list above?

Are there any additional agreements that you would like to add to the list?

# Addiction

A person can be addicted to a substance, such as alcohol, heroin, opiates or opioids, caffeine, tobacco, and sugar. A person also can be addicted to a behavior, such as shopping, exercising, gambling, having sex, viewing pornography, and using social media.

One of the authors of this program, Dr. Stephanie Covington, defines addiction as: "The chronic neglect of self in favor of something or someone else." In other words, the focus of our addiction consumes our attention, our time, and our energy to the point where we begin neglecting all other aspects of our lives. You will find that this program focuses a lot on issues of the self, because so many people have lost themselves in their addictive disorders. Here are some of the key things to remember about addiction, also known as the ABCDEs, from the American Society of Addiction Medicine:

A.  The person is not able to *abstain*
B.  The person has reduced *behavioral* control
C.  The person has a *craving* or increased "hunger" for drugs or addictive experiences
D.  The person has *diminished* recognition of significant problems with personal behaviors and interpersonal relationships
E.  The person has a dysfunctional *emotional* response

The American Society of Addiction Medicine defines addiction as a chronic disease involving the circuits of the brain that deal with reward, motivation, and memory. When there is a problem with these circuits, there are biological, psychological, social, and spiritual difficulties. A person with an addiction pursues reward and/or relief by substance use and other behaviors. Like other chronic diseases, addiction often involves cycles of relapse and remission. The Society says, "Without treatment or engagement in recovery activities, addiction is progressive and can result in disability or premature death."

# Trauma

According to the U.S. Substance Abuse and Mental Health Services Administration, "trauma results from an event, series of events, or set of circumstances that is experienced by an individual as physically or emotionally harmful or threatening and that has lasting adverse effects on the individual's functioning and physical, social, emotional, or spiritual well-being." In Greek, trauma means "wound."

Every human being experiences difficult, painful, and even devastating events. Some of these events leave emotional wounds. We all heal from those wounds differently. If their wounds don't heal properly, some people turn to alcohol or other drugs or other addictive behaviors as a way of managing painful memories and feelings. Those behaviors frequently lead to even more trauma and pain. Trauma and addiction often go hand in hand. In trying to deal with our wounds by ourselves, we sometimes make the situation worse.

There are many types of violence and other experiences that can create trauma, including:

- Abandonment or neglect (especially for small children)
- Emotional, sexual, or physical abuse during childhood
- Witnessing violence between parents or household members
- Domestic violence
- Kidnapping
- Getting kicked out of the house and/or living on the streets
- Being rejected by family members, friends, or a religious community because of your sexuality, gender expression, or gender identity
- Loss of a loved one (family member, friend, mentor, colleague, or pet)
- Rape or sexual assault
- Being outed (having your sexuality or gender identity shared) without your consent
- Being deadnamed (for trans and nonbinary people, having people use your birth name instead of your chosen name)
- Witnessing murder

- Gang activity
- Mugging, robbery
- Being arrested and/or experiencing violence at the hands of law enforcement
- Accidents (automobile, bicycle, falls, work-related)
- Medical abuse (not receiving medications or procedures you need, conversion therapy)
- Serious injuries and illnesses (sports-related, gunshot wounds, cancer, cardiac/heart conditions)
- Extremely painful and/or frightening medical procedures
- War and combat
- Immigration-related stresses, such as ICE raids, refugee journeys, or living as an undocumented person
- Intergenerational (cultural or historical) trauma
- Climate trauma and natural disasters (earthquakes, hurricanes, tornadoes, fires, floods)

In the case of a natural disaster, people often gather around the victims, there is acknowledgment of what happened, and sympathy and comfort may be offered. Other forms of trauma, like war and terrorism, elicit clear reactions and are identified immediately as trauma. That is very different from what often happens after traumas such as assault, incest, rape, and domestic violence. These experiences often are hidden, and the victims rarely get to publicly acknowledge what took place and receive the support they deserve and need to move on in their lives. Too often, the victim of a secret trauma ends up with a deep sense of shame and invisibility, along with silent rage associated with not being acknowledged or protected. Many incidents of childhood abuse are perpetrated by adults who were supposed to love and protect. Therefore, the pain of the abuse is magnified by the betrayal of trust.

*Helping Men Recover* is for people who have addictive disorders and for those who also may have experienced threatening events—including suffering inflicted by others—that have overwhelmed their psychological and/or physiological coping mechanisms. We ask that you keep an open mind about how trauma may have affected your life. Whatever pain you may be living with, you deserve to heal.

The downward spiral represents the limitations and constrictions that addiction can create in a person's life. The line through the middle represents the object of the

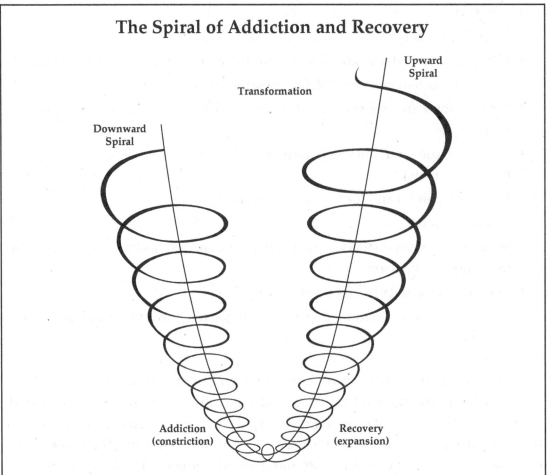

## The Spiral of Addiction and Recovery

Upward Spiral

Transformation

Downward Spiral

Addiction (constriction)

Recovery (expansion)

Source: *Helping Women Recover: A Program for Treating Addiction* (rev. ed.), by Stephanie S. Covington, 2019. San Francisco, CA: Jossey-Bass. Copyright 2008 by Stephanie S. Covington. Reprinted with permission.

person's addiction. It can be alcohol, heroin, gambling, or any other behavior that the person has become dependent on. It becomes the organizing principle in the person's life. Everything else becomes secondary to the substance or the behavior, and the person's life becomes smaller and smaller.

This program represents a turning point, perhaps at the bottom of the downward spiral. The person steps onto a new path, the upward spiral. It represents the process of recovery, in which the person's life begins to expand. The addiction is still the line through the middle, but it has less influence; it has loosened its grip. There is space now for new activities and new relationships. The experience of addiction becomes just one thread in the tapestry of life; it is no longer the core. It becomes just one of many life experiences. The image of the spiral helps us to see that recovery is a transformative process. As people sustain their recovery, they are able to say, "Who I am today is not who I was."

If you are working this program alone, it may help to ask a friend or counselor to read the instructions to you the first time or two you do any of the grounding activities, to help you become familiar with them.

# Breathing

1. Stand with your feet a little distance apart so that you feel stable. Take a few deep breaths.
2. Relax your shoulders and drop your hands to your sides. Let your arms and hands just dangle, relaxed. Relax your shoulders and arms.
3. Take in a long deep breath through your nose and blow it out through your mouth like a big gust of wind or like blowing out a candle.
4. Now inhale again as if you are smelling a rose and then let the air out by blowing it out of your mouth.
5. Remember to relax your shoulders and arms.
6. Do the inhaling and exhaling three more times.

# Focusing on the Here and Now

1. Relax. Take a deep breath.
2. Look at the room around you. Focus on the size of the room.
3. Focus on:
   - the color and texture of the walls
   - the height of the ceilings
   - the lights
   - the windows [if there are any]
   - the doors
   - the furniture
   - the decorations
4. Now focus on yourself.
   - Think of your name.
   - Think of your age.
   - Think of today's date and what time it is.
   - Think of what city and state you are in.
   - Think of the program you are in with this group.

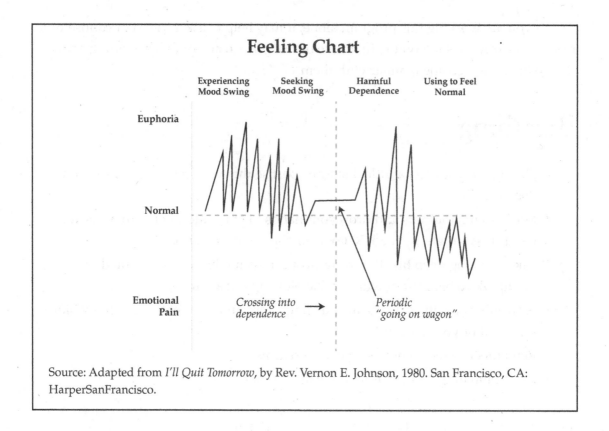

**Feeling Chart**

Experiencing Mood Swing — Seeking Mood Swing — Harmful Dependence — Using to Feel Normal

Euphoria

Normal

Emotional Pain

*Crossing into dependence* →

*Periodic "going on wagon"*

Source: Adapted from *I'll Quit Tomorrow*, by Rev. Vernon E. Johnson, 1980. San Francisco, CA: HarperSanFrancisco.

This chart traces the progression of addiction on an emotional level.

1. The first reaction is *experiencing* the mood swing that is brought about by the addictive substance or behavior. At this early stage, the swing is in the positive direction and is pleasant. The person experiments with dosage—the amount of the drug or behavior—and is learning to control the degree of the mood swing in this way.

2. Next comes *seeking* the mood swing and looking forward to it. The person's behavior becomes directed toward experiencing euphoria. At this stage, for example, drinkers or drug users are waiting for the party or the fix, and gamblers are looking forward to the casino or racetrack. They are needing more and more of the substance or behavior in order to get the good feelings. Some mood-swing experiences begin to be physically negative, including hangovers, feeling nauseated, losing money, and embarrassment at reports of their behavior. Because the swing back to normal can still be made, they are not paying a significant emotional price yet.

3. At the stage of *harmful dependence,* an invisible line is crossed between misuse and actual dependence or addiction. Drinking or using for pleasure, for the fun of the mood swing, is no longer primary. Much of the time it is just to reduce the stress of not having the drug or doing the behavior. The emotional cost is increasingly great. When the addicted person swings back, often they are unable to make it back to normal. They are in pain and have lost control, yet they may be unaware that they are in trouble. Typical indicators of harmful dependence or addiction include these indicators of a downward progression:

    • Obsession, meaning that a person's thoughts are constantly directed toward the addictive substance or behavior;

    • Compulsion, meaning that the person's behavior is directed toward the addiction most of the time;

    • Increased tolerance, meaning that the person needs more and more of the substance or the behavior to obtain the same effect;

    • Decreased tolerance, meaning that the person is no longer able to use as much alcohol or other drugs;

    • Anxious protection of the supply, meaning fear of running out; and

    • Withdrawal, meaning negative physical symptoms when the supply is not available.

4. The fourth and final stage is *using to feel normal.* The person is in a state of chronic emotional pain and depression. The behavior originally aimed at feeling euphoric no longer provides a high. The person is just trying to feel normal.

# Between-Sessions Activities

1. Because *Helping Men Recover* can be used to explore a variety of addictive behaviors, it will be helpful for you to identify clearly what addiction you are working on. *If you are concerned about several drugs or behaviors, please choose one or two to focus on.* Some examples are

   □ alcohol

   □ heroin

   □ cocaine

   □ methamphetamine

   □ opiates or opioids

   □ prescription drugs

- [ ] other drug(s) _____
- [ ] caffeine
- [ ] tobacco
- [ ] sugar
- [ ] shopping (in real life, on television [for example, QVC], or online)
- [ ] exercising
- [ ] gambling
- [ ] having sex
- [ ] viewing pornography
- [ ] using social media
- [ ] other behavior _____

2. On the downward part of the spiral illustration on page 10, make a list of the constrictions or limitations created in your life by your addiction. On the upward spiral, look into the future and see what tools and experiences you think will get you to your best self. If you have had a previous recovery, think about that and add whatever you wish.

3. The other activity for you to do between now and our next session is to practice the two grounding activities you learned today: Breathing and Exhaling and Focusing on the Here and Now. Try to do each of them at least once each day between now and our next session.

# Recovery Breathing

1. Take a deep breath in through your nose.
2. Hold it.
3. Now let the air out through your mouth.
4. Do this three more times.
5. As you breathe in through your nose, breathe in all of the support and love you need for your recovery.
6. As you breathe out, let go of anything that is getting in the way of your recovery.
7. Again, breathe in all the love and support you need, hold it, and then breathe out any barriers to your recovery. Do this one more time.

# Reflections on Recovery

In the space below, please write any thoughts, feelings, or questions that you might have about what was covered in the Opening Session.

# MODULE A

# Self

Beginning a process of recovery entails discovering oneself. The self is what is unique about each individual. It is the part of a person that says I am, I feel, I like, I want, and I know. Identifying ourselves helps us to organize our experiences and make sense of our reality. It gives purpose and direction to our choices and behavior.

Addiction cuts us off from our true selves. It numbs and confuses us, so that we don't know who we are; what we feel; or what we like, want, or know. Recovery is a process of finding, knowing, and caring for the self in a deep and powerful way. In the recovery process, people grow less dependent on the objects of addiction.

This first module, Self, focuses on your identity, including an exploration of your inner life—your thoughts and feelings. These are areas that you may have ignored, avoided, or hidden from view for years. This module is designed to help begin the journey of discovering who you are beyond your traditional roles, how you came to be the person you are today, and what kind of person you would like to be in the future.

You also will have the opportunity to learn grounding and relaxation techniques that you can use whenever you feel stressed; how you can improve your ability to communicate with others respectfully, openly, and honestly; and that having feelings is a normal and natural aspect of being human.

Remember, when you begin to use this workbook after a group session or on your own, take a minute or two to unwind, relax, and focus on where you are now. Just get settled in the way that feels best for you. Allow yourself to notice how you're breathing and then inhale gently and exhale fully. Repeat the breathing exercise two more times. If you experience difficult feelings during the program, try using one of the grounding activities that you will be learning in the sessions.

# Defining Self

In the process of recovery, you will ask the question "Who am I?" many times. This will take you on a journey of exploring your inner feelings, thoughts, and beliefs, as well as looking at your relationships and the roles you play. Each time, you grow closer to knowing who you really are and have another chance to let go of who you are not. Although each of us is affected by our past experiences, in recovery we get the opportunity to reinvent ourselves. You get to decide what kind of person you want to be from here on.

The goals of this session are

1. To begin to explore the question "Who am I?"
2. To learn that we are more than what we do
3. To realize that self-discovery is a lifelong task

## Feeling Okay: Grounding and Relaxation Activities

There are times when you may feel uncomfortable or anxious in the group or in any unfamiliar setting or situation. This happens to all of us at times. Most of the time, we

*A Man's Workbook: Helping Men Recover, A Program for Treating Addiction*, Second Edition.
Stephanie S. Covington, Dan Griffin, and Rick Dauer.
© 2022 Stephanie S. Covington, Dan Griffin, and Rick Dauer. Published 2022 by John Wiley & Sons, Inc.

keep these feelings to ourselves and do not know how to relieve our discomfort, so we turn to alcohol and other drugs.

Here are three techniques that you can use to help you to relax or calm yourself and feel more grounded. Being grounded means being able to stay in the present, without focusing on the past or the future. It also means not having your emotions run the show, including emotional memories and fears. These techniques can help you to detach from your emotional discomfort by becoming more aware of the physical world, to be present in the here and now. These grounding activities will help you to deal with your feelings so that they do not control your behavior and take you back to using.

## Palms Up/Palms Down

1. Sit up straight in your seat, with both feet on the floor and your eyes closed or your eyelids lowered so that you are not distracted.
2. Hold both your arms outstretched, with the palms of your hands turned up and touching side by side, as though someone was about to put something in your hands.
3. Visualize a list of all the thoughts and feelings that are bothering you right now.
4. Now imagine placing all your cares, concerns, problems, troubles, and painful memories into your hands. All these negative emotions and thoughts are out of your bodies and lying in your hands.
5. Imagine the weight of holding all these problems, these negative thoughts and emotions, in your hands. Feel the strain of carrying them.
6. Go back inside yourself and find any remaining pain, discomfort, and stress. Then slowly move these sensations out through your arms and into your hands.
7. You may feel the weight of the emotional and physical distress pushing down on your hands.
8. Now, slowly and carefully turn your hands upside down, so that your palms face the floor. Let all the problems, stresses, bad feelings, and negativity fall to the floor. For now, drop your burdens.
9. Finally, open your eyes and bring your attention back to the present.

## Relaxation

1. Relax again. Take a deep breath. Let it out.
2. You are going to tense up certain parts of your body and then let the tension go. If you want to make a sound when you are letting the tension go, that may help you to connect more to your body.
3. Hold your hands out in front of you. Make a fist as tight as you can.

*Helping Men Recover A Man's Workbook*

4. Now, open your hands and let them relax.

5. Now tense your arms.

6. And relax.

7. Now tense your feet.

8. And relax.

9. Tense your legs.

10. And relax.

11. Tense your stomach.

12. And relax.

13. Tense your chest and your back.

14. And relax.

15. Tense your jaw.

16. And relax.

17. Tense the muscles in your face.

18. And relax.

19. Now see if you can tense your whole body.

20. And relax it.

## Deep Breathing

1. Put one hand on your chest and one hand on your stomach.

2. Take a couple of normal breaths. You probably will find that you are feeling these breaths mostly in your chest.

3. Try moving your breath deeper into your lower abdomen, so that your hand on your stomach moves as you breathe.

4. Close your mouth and press your tongue lightly to the roof of your mouth. Let your jaw relax.

5. Take a breath slowly in through your nose, counting to three.

6. Slowly exhale and feel the breath leaving your nose as you count to three one more time.

7. This activity is called "Deep Breathing." Try it again.

8. You will find that you are breathing more slowly and more completely than usual. As thoughts come up, acknowledge them and then return your focus to your breathing.

9. Keep breathing deeply, but blow the air out of your mouth, rather than out of your nose. Let your abdomen fill with air each time.

# Possibilities Page

It is important to learn to experience and acknowledge our feelings. The following list on the left can help you to practice answering the question, "How am I feeling today?" You also will use this list in a later activity called "Who Am I?"

| Feelings | Beliefs | Qualities |
|---|---|---|
| angry | honesty is the best policy | sense of humor |
| joyful | family is important | dependable |
| sad | loyalty is important | sincere |
| anxious | hard work is good for you | good natured |
| thoughtful | monogamy is best | trustworthy |
| nervous | there is a God | smart |
| happy | save the earth | compassionate |
| afraid | save money | streetwise |
| amused | stay young at heart | gentle |
| hurt | fatherhood is fun | strong |
| bitter | life is tough | creative |
| jealous | expect the best | survivor |
| calm | you are what you eat | wise |
| lonely | anger is dangerous | funny |
| mad | have safe sex | warm |
| contented | reincarnation happens | honest |
| miserable | don't trust the government | passionate |
| disappointed | think before you speak | calm |
| pleased | trust your friends | sensible |
| overjoyed | better safe than sorry | energetic |
| discouraged | I'm full of ideas | reliable |
| depressed | I'm good with words | encouraging |
| relieved | I'm good with pictures | open |
| glad | I'm good with numbers | truthful |
| disturbed | I'm good at making things | perceptive |
| embarrassed | I'm a good listener | mellow |
| furious | money can't buy happiness | curious |
| grateful | live one day at a time | cynical |
| hopeful | anything can happen | timid |
| worried | don't sweat the small stuff | brave |

*Helping Men Recover A Man's Workbook*

# What Do You Want to Get Out of This Group?

You are probably using this workbook because alcohol or other drugs have been causing you serious problems. You may be in this program because you were court-ordered to treatment or in order to reduce your sentence. How you got here is not as important as what you choose to do now. Recovery is about taking responsibility for how you feel, how you act, and how you relate with others. This program will help you realize that, although you can't always control what happens to you, you do get to decide what kind of person you become.

Please think about what you want to get out of the group experience. If you are using this workbook by yourself, think of what your goal is. Think about what *you* really want, not what your counselor, a judge, your partner, your parole or probation officer, or anyone else wants. What do you need to accomplish in order to become the person you always knew you could be? Sobriety is a great answer but it should not be your only answer.

1. What do you want to get out of this program?

2. What do you think you will need from the rest of the group in order to get what you want?

3. What can you do to help yourself get what you want?

# Who Am I?

Most of us have been taught to think of ourselves in terms of our roles as providers, fathers, husbands, relationship partners, employees, teammates, and so on. There is nothing wrong with this—in fact, our connections with others tell us much about who we are. However, our roles do not tell the whole story about who we are. In recovery, it is important to develop our relationships with others—our outer selves—and our relationship with our inner selves—our thoughts, feelings, values, and beliefs.

We are often uncomfortable focusing on our relationships and our inner selves. We may have been brought up to consider these things to not be masculine. So, we ignore how we feel and how the other people in our lives feel. We focus on work, sports, or possessions and tend to define ourselves according to our successes in these areas.

The questions in this section will help you begin to get to know yourself and your fellow group members better.

1. Think back to when you were about ten years old. How would someone who knew you at that age have described you?

2. Think of three things about you that answer the question "Who am I?"
   Here's the hard part: none of your answers can refer to your work or your
   identity as a partner, lover, friend, or family member. This isn't about the
   sports you play or your favorite leisure activities. This isn't about your
   interactions with others or who you think you are supposed to be; it's about
   who you are on the inside. Our inner selves are made up of our thoughts,
   feelings, values, and beliefs. Think about qualities or characteristics
   that you have.

   Refer back to the Possibilities Page. It lists a number of feelings, beliefs,
   and personal qualities. Many of us find it hard to talk about who we are because
   we can't think of words for these things; we don't yet possess the language.
   Look at the list and see if you can find up to three words each that describe

   • Feelings you are currently experiencing

   • Beliefs that you have

   • Qualities that you possess

Answering these questions is a good start in exploring your inner self. As you continue in this program, you will learn much more about who you are and who you want to be.

# Gender and Gender Expression

Gender *identity* is about how one views oneself and who one is as far as being masculine or feminine or neither. Gender *expression* is how one expresses one's gender. The way that gender has commonly been depicted in the United States is that you are one of two things: male or female—what we call "binary" or having only two options. Today, gender is understood more as a continuum, and people can express themselves with or without gendered characteristics or with any combination of them. They may express themselves differently in different situations or at different times in their lives.

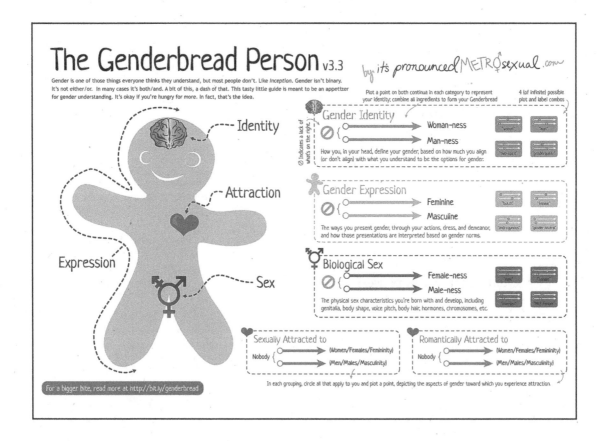

# Between-Sessions Activity

## Recovery Scale: Self

Please take a few moments to mark the degree to which you do each of the following things. Make an "X" or a circle on each line to indicate your response. You will complete this form again at the end of this module on Self to see how you have changed. You will not have to compare your answers with anyone else's, and you will not be judged on how well you are doing. This is not a test, but an opportunity for you to chart your own progress in recovery.

| | Not at All | Just a Little | Pretty Much | Very Much |
|---|---|---|---|---|
| 1. I keep up my physical appearance (bathing, hair, clean clothes, nails). | | | | |
| 2. I exercise regularly. | | | | |
| 3. I eat healthy meals. | | | | |
| 4. I get restful sleep. | | | | |
| 5. I go to work/school (or I complete required tasks). | | | | |
| 6. I can adapt to change. | | | | |
| 7. I keep up my living space. | | | | |
| 8. I take constructive criticism well. | | | | |
| 9. I can accept praise. | | | | |
| 10. I laugh at funny things. | | | | |
| 11. I acknowledge my needs and feelings. | | | | |
| 12. I engage in new interests. | | | | |
| 13. I can relax without alcohol or other drugs. | | | | |
| 14. I value myself. | | | | |

# Reflections on Recovery

In the space below, please write any thoughts, feelings, or questions that you might have about what was covered in this session.

# Men in Recovery

Most of us grow up being told how we are supposed to think and feel and act. We don't spend a lot of time thinking about the traditional assumptions and expectations in our society about masculinity or our beliefs about what it means to be a man. We learn these ideas from our parents, other family members, teachers, coaches, friends, the street, books, movies, television shows, social media, and so on. If we see others not following the rules, we may humiliate and even abuse them.

If being sober is your priority, you will benefit from looking at how some ideas about masculinity could affect your recovery. Some of these ideas may be healthy and productive for you, and some of them may impair your ability to stay sober and fully realize your potential. Some beliefs that work for you may not work for others.

The goals of this session are

- To understand our ideas about masculinity and where we learned them
- To explore the basic principles of recovery
- To recognize that traditional notions of masculinity may affect a person's response to the process of early recovery

*A Man's Workbook: Helping Men Recover, A Program for Treating Addiction*, Second Edition.
Stephanie S. Covington, Dan Griffin, and Rick Dauer.
© 2022 Stephanie S. Covington, Dan Griffin, and Rick Dauer. Published 2022 by John Wiley & Sons, Inc.

# "The Man Rules" and the Principles of Recovery

There are many "rules" for being a man in our society. We learn them from our families, our friends, our schools, our communities and churches, the media, and other places. Examples are: "boys don't cry," "men don't admit weakness or fear," and "men don't ask for help." One of the rules is that we need to be in control: of our emotions, our relationships, and so on. Fear of losing control may lead to dishonesty; aggressive or violent behavior; and self-destructive acts, such as overuse of alcohol and other drugs. Of course, we often cannot control other people or external events. We may not be able to control what we think or feel, but we have a great deal of control over how we respond and how we act.

Not all of the beliefs about and rules for being a man in our society work for us in recovery. Some of them do. But sometimes we misunderstand a rule or we take its value to an extreme. These sessions help you to start thinking more consciously about your beliefs about being a man, so that you can choose what kind of man you want to be. You at least will be more aware of the assumptions and choices you make.

1. In the space that follows, list all the "rules" about being a man that you can come up with. Examples are: "Men should never show weakness" and "Men should take care of their partners."

2. Now think about what it means to be in recovery. This may still be a new concept for you, but recovery is going to be the foundation of your new life. From what has been discussed in the group and what you have learned in other treatment groups or at any Twelve Step meetings, what do you think are the main principles of being in recovery? What do you need to do to stay sober? Examples are: "It's important to build a support system and use it" and "It's necessary to accept responsibility for my actions." In the space that follows, list as many principles of recovery as you can.

3. In order to be in recovery, you may be asked to do some things that conflict with your ideas about what is manly. You will have to choose whether being sober is more important than following the "rules" that you have learned without questioning them.

• Which rules for being a man support recovery?

• Which rules for being a man do not support recovery?

*Helping Men Recover A Man's Workbook*

# Between-Sessions Activity

1. On the pages before this, be sure to list The Man Rules that apply most to you, adding any new ones that your group (or you) didn't come up with.

2. Then, thinking about how some of the rules support recovery and some of them do not, write down which of the rules about being a man you are willing to change and which ones you want to keep for now. Use the space below to record your answers. Please be prepared to discuss your efforts at the beginning of the next session.

   - Which of The Man Rules are you willing to change?

   - Which of them do you want to keep for now?

Recovery is a process, and no one is asking you to become a different person overnight. But we do encourage you to try out new behaviors and ideas. You may find that these suit you better than the ones you've held on to for a long time.

# Reflections on Recovery

In the space below, please write any thoughts, feelings, or questions that you might have about what was covered in this session.

# SESSION 4

# A Sense of Self

Who we are at any point in time is a combination of the people, events, and experiences that have played roles in our lives. We can think of our lives as journeys from birth to where we are now and to where we will be in the future.

Your past has shaped you but it doesn't have to control you. You can shape your present and future through the choices you make from now on.

The goals of this session are

- To gain a better sense of who we are today by exploring our pasts
- To understand that our lives are like stories, with pasts, presents, and futures
- To recognize that, to a large degree, we get to be the authors of our life stories
- To gain understanding and respect for one another by hearing how our stories are alike and how they are different

*A Man's Workbook: Helping Men Recover, A Program for Treating Addiction,* Second Edition.
Stephanie S. Covington, Dan Griffin, and Rick Dauer.
© 2022 Stephanie S. Covington, Dan Griffin, and Rick Dauer. Published 2022 by John Wiley & Sons, Inc.

# Looking Back: Your Journey

Who we are at any point in time is a combination of the people, events, and experiences that have played roles in our lives since birth. We can think of our lives as journeys from birth to where we are now and to where we will be in the future. The landmarks of our journeys are

- People we have encountered along the way, such as mothers, fathers, grandparents, teachers, sexual partners, friends, spouses, and co-workers
- Events we have been involved in, including one-time occurrences, such as births, accidents, and graduations
- Experiences we have had (for example, isolation in high school, summers away from home, being drunk or high, and being arrested)

Exploring who we are today entails going back and looking at the people, events, and experiences that have shaped us. Sometimes looking at the past can be painful. We've experienced and done a lot of things that we'd rather forget. But remembering is important because, if we're cut off from our pasts, we're cut off from essential parts of our selves.

Also, examining our pasts can help us to identify things that we want to be different in the future. The good news is that we can make choices today that will improve our lives six months or a year from now. The past has shaped us but it doesn't necessarily have to control us. We can even begin to see the past differently. With distance and healing, we can have new ideas about our pasts. We can shape the present and our futures through the choices that we make today and every day hereafter.

On the pages that follow, make some notes about the people, events, and experiences that have played major parts in creating who you are today. Write down key words and phrases or draw pictures or symbols that portray the major people, events, and experiences of your life. Consider both the positive and negative aspects of your past.

# People

---

**Some examples:**

*My dad—an angry and violent man*

*The guys I met in the Army*

*My first girlfriend, who broke my heart*

---

# Events

> ## Some examples:
>
> *My first sexual experience*
>
> *Buying our first house*
>
> *Being arrested and going to jail*

# Experiences

> **Some examples:**
>
> *Moving around a lot as a child*
>
> *Becoming addicted to pain medications*
>
> *Going back to school and starting a new career*

# Our Life Journeys

1. Now that you have heard the group members' stories, what are some ways in which your story and theirs are alike? What do you have in common?

2. In what ways are your stories different? What makes each of you unique? What are some of the differences in the members of your group?

3. When you think back over your life story, what are some of the strengths you've developed? You can answer this question even if you are using this workbook individually.

# Between-Sessions Activities

1. Think about how you would like to define yourself and write the answers on this page. One way to think about this would be to think of what you would like people to say about you at your funeral.

2. You may also want to continue to practice the grounding activities that you have been doing at the beginning of each session.

# Reflections on Recovery

In the space below, please write any thoughts, feelings, or questions that you might have about what was covered in this session.

# Men: Inside and Out

We are all composed of the selves we show to the world (our "outer selves" or the "outsides" of our houses) and the selves we keep from almost everyone else (our "inner selves" or the "insides" of our houses). Our inner selves consist of our thoughts, feelings, values, and beliefs.

We keep our outer selves (the outsides of our houses) looking a certain way, because these are what we show to others. We create our images through our behaviors, possessions, clothes, and relationships. We want others to admire us, so we try to present what we think are desired images to the rest of the world or to the environment that we are currently living in.

The chances are that you have paid a lot more attention to the outside of your house than to the inside. But *you* have to live inside your house, and when you don't take care of it, it's hard for you to stay healthy. Addiction makes a mess of the inside, and you may come to believe that you don't deserve any better.

It can be tough to look at the inner parts of ourselves, especially the parts that we keep from others. A lot of us simply ignore our inner houses, hoping that all the time, effort, and money we invest in the outsides will compensate for what's missing on the inside. But the more attention you give to the inside of your house (the inner you), the more comfortable you will feel inviting others in to be with you. Recovery works best from the inside out. In other words, it's impossible to be okay with others until we are okay with ourselves.

*A Man's Workbook: Helping Men Recover, A Program for Treating Addiction*, Second Edition.
Stephanie S. Covington, Dan Griffin, and Rick Dauer.
© 2022 Stephanie S. Covington, Dan Griffin, and Rick Dauer. Published 2022 by John Wiley & Sons, Inc.

The goals of this session are

- To understand how messages from our culture, our families, and our peers shape the ways in which we see ourselves
- To understand that a person is often two different people: the one on the outside who is shown to others and the one on the inside who experiences life primarily through feelings often hidden from others
- To become more comfortable acknowledging and expressing our feelings

# My House, Outside and Inside

On the following pages are drawings of two houses. The first drawing represents the outside of your house: that part of yourself that you show to the world. Write descriptions of the way you think others see you. Describe what you and other people see when they look at your exterior. This description should have positive as well as negative things.

Here are some possible things to consider when doing the outside of your house:

- How do you act around strangers?
- What kind of clothes, shoes, jewelry, and other apparel do you like to wear?
- Are you quiet, argumentative, polite, vulgar, generous?
- What does the outside of your house say about you? What do you consider to be the qualities that you try to communicate to others?
- What is the image you try to develop to impress others?

The second drawing represents the inside of your house: the thoughts, feelings, beliefs, and personal qualities that you may keep to yourself, hidden from view. Write about who you are on the inside. What don't other people see?

Here are some possible things to consider when doing the inside of your house:

- What have been some of your hopes and dreams?
- What words or phrases would you use to describe who you are?
- What are some of your values or beliefs?
- What are you proud of about yourself?
- What are some of the things about your life that you regret?

Try to make sure that neither the outside nor inside of your house shows all positive or all negative attributes. We are all some combination of both.

# The outside of your house

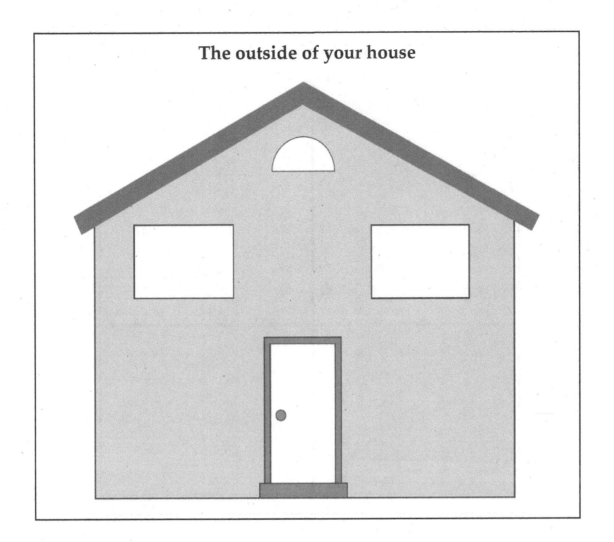

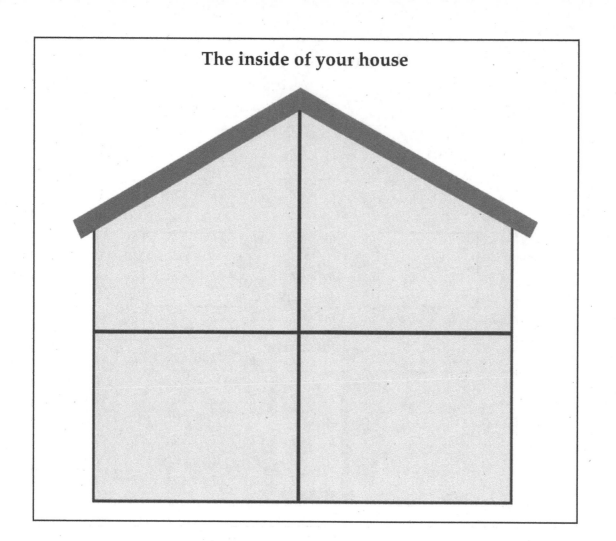

**The inside of your house**

# Discussion Questions

1. What did you put on the outside of your house?

2. What did you include inside your house?

3. What do you think works for you regarding the outside of your house? What doesn't work for you?

4. What would it take for you to feel more comfortable sharing your inner world with others? If you are in a group program, how can the members of your subgroup help you feel more trusting and safer?

# The Emotions Game

There are six emotions written on the front of your card. On the back of your card, you will write the names of six people who are (or have been) important figures in your life. A person may be a parent, sibling, other relative, friend, coach, teacher, co-worker, intimate partner, and so on. A person may be living or may be deceased.

Here is a sample card:

| **The Emotions Game** | |
|---|---|
| 1. Love | 1. _Mom_ |
| 2. Fear | 2. _Eli_ |
| 3. Anger | 3. _Damian_ |
| 4. Shame | 4. _Mr. Jones_ |
| 5. Joy | 5. _Coach Rodriguez_ |
| 6. Sadness | 6. _Gloria_ |

If you are using this workbook alone, pick one of the emotions to put next to each name (a different emotion for each different name), and make some notes about why you associate that person with that emotion. For example, if the person is your older sister, and the emotion you picked for her is love, think about a time when you had strong feelings of love for your sister or you were made aware of her strong feelings of love for you.

# Between-Sessions Activity

Between now and our next session, do something that will improve the inside of your house. Some examples are writing a list of all your resentments, going to an extra support-group meeting, thinking about how to make amends to someone you may have harmed, or making a commitment to be more honest with others.

# Reflections on Recovery

In the space below, please write any thoughts, feelings, or questions that you might have about what was covered in this session.

# Men and Feelings

We all experience a range of feelings, including fear, sadness, hurt, joy, shame, loneliness, and anger. How we feel is no indication of our "manliness." Feelings are there to help us experience life more fully. They are essential parts of who we are. When we ignore our feelings or are disconnected from them, we miss out on important parts of life. It also can harm our relationships and our health.

The activities that you have done in the past sessions have brought up feelings for you, whether you were aware of them or not. The feelings, or your awareness of them, may not have surfaced until later in the day or even another day.

Communicating your feelings may not be easy or comfortable for you. It will benefit you to allow yourself to experience your feelings and to make the effort to share them with a person you trust, as long as you do it in a safe way. The more you do this, the more comfortable you will be on the "inside of your house." This also increases your sense of connection with yourself and others that is the foundation of healthy and rewarding relationships.

Expressing your feelings may result in you becoming very vulnerable in certain environments, such as correctional facilities. Perhaps you have found that anger is a way to protect yourself emotionally and even physically. So, go at your own pace but work toward becoming more comfortable in acknowledging and honoring what you are experiencing on an emotional level.

*A Man's Workbook: Helping Men Recover, A Program for Treating Addiction*, Second Edition.
Stephanie S. Covington, Dan Griffin, and Rick Dauer.
© 2022 Stephanie S. Covington, Dan Griffin, and Rick Dauer. Published 2022 by John Wiley & Sons, Inc.

The goals of this session are

- To increase our understanding of how acknowledging and sharing our feelings will help define who we are
- To begin to understand the role that anger plays in our lives and the idea of the "anger funnel"
- To recognize that healthy relationships rely on the effective communication of inner thoughts and feelings

# Relationships and Feelings: Discussion Questions

1. What role do you think your feelings have played in your addiction?

2. How have your feelings and your ability to share them affected your close relationships?

3. What have been the positive effects in your relationships?

4. What have been the negative effects?

# The Anger Funnel

Most of us had a turning point early in our lives when we realized that it is not okay—or even safe—to express fear, hurt, or sadness. So anger is the only feeling that many men allow themselves. Then they think they will be safe—both because they are expressing an "acceptable" emotion and because anger may intimidate others or keep them at a distance.

Others avoid anger for fear that they'll lose their temper or perhaps even become violent. They may live in a state of resentment because they never express their anger (and maybe any other feeling).

The truth is that often the real emotion is not anger. Most anger is what we call a "surface" or "secondary" emotion. There often is a more genuine feeling underneath. For example, imagine that you and a friend are having an argument. Your friend calls you a rude name and then makes fun of your social background. Other examples are if you get passed up for a promotion or if a friend doesn't return your phone calls. Most of us are conditioned to respond with anger. But if we look closer, we can recognize that what we are really feeling is another emotion: hurt, fear, loss, uncertainty, shame, sorrow, or frustration. A lot of anger is about a fear of loss—of love or respect or power or something else. If men have been taught that it is not okay—or even safe—to express fear, hurt, shame, or sadness, they substitute anger.

The Anger Funnel is a representation of how our true feelings are transformed into anger. We pour all our emotions into this funnel, and anger is the only thing that

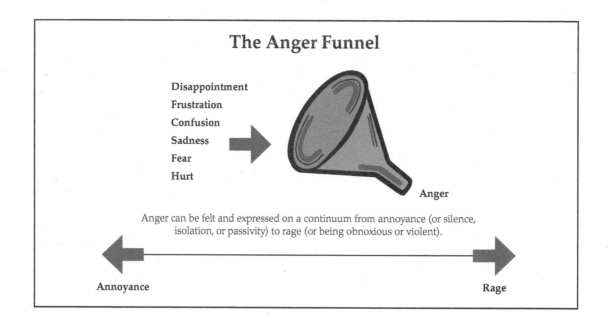

**The Anger Funnel**

Disappointment
Frustration
Confusion
Sadness
Fear
Hurt

Anger

Anger can be felt and expressed on a continuum from annoyance (or silence, isolation, or passivity) to rage (or being obnoxious or violent).

Annoyance

Rage

comes out the other end. Anger becomes a protective shield. We never talk about or deal with the underlying emotions.

Of course, there are times when anger is the appropriate emotion, such as when your rights or your safety have been violated. The question is about how we express our anger and whether we act on it in a way that harms other people.

## Shame

Shame is that deeply held belief that there is something wrong with us. We're not smart enough, or lovable enough, or attractive enough. Shame is about not feeling worthwhile at our cores. Shame can be the result of growing up in a challenging family system, when we thought that the neglect or abuse we experienced was because there was something wrong with us. It also can result from the choices we make and the behaviors we engage in. If we violate our value systems once or twice, we may feel guilt or remorse. If we violate our value systems regularly, we are likely to feel shame, which is a deeper and more lasting emotion. Alcoholism and addiction are considered shame-based diseases. When we're drunk or high, and act in ways that are in direct opposition to our values, later we may experience a feeling of shame. And what makes uncomfortable feelings like shame go away? More drinking or drug use, of course.

When shame is the predominant emotion being fed into the Anger Funnel, there is a good chance that rage and even violence will emerge at the bottom.

## Rage

We need to distinguish between anger and rage. Rage is a destructive feeling that often results from feeling shame or out of control. Rage can cause serious harm, particularly when it is expressed through abusive or violent behavior.

The other emotion that is likely to turn into rage is fear. Rage makes us feel strong and powerful. We may direct that rage toward the person who caused us to feel fear, or we may direct it toward someone else whom we think we can dominate.

# Communication and Feelings

There are communication patterns that limit or constrict us emotionally. Many of these are learned in our families, and we take those patterns into our future relationships. Emotional constriction also can result from addiction, abuse, and experiencing a traumatic event.

1. *Not speaking.* When you don't speak, you start to assume things about other people. You rely on other cues to tell you about a person's mood, thoughts, and so on. In dysfunctional or abusive families, kids learn to "read" or assume or guess what is going on, because adults do not communicate directly and openly. Relying on nonverbal communication without checking out assumptions creates misunderstandings and disconnection between people.

2. *Non-risky facts.* Some families talk only about safe or non-risky subjects. This form of communication is a way to stay safe and avoid conflict or unpleasant emotions, but it limits people's connections to one another.

3. *Offering opinions.* Opinions are important, but they need to be communicated as opinions rather than as facts. Otherwise, conversations tend to become adversarial, and people feel that they are not being heard.

4. *"Poor me, ain't it awful" stories.* Some people want to believe, and have others believe, that they often are victims of unfair treatment. They do not accept responsibility for their problems and, therefore, are unlikely to make any attempt to change.

When children grow up in families that communicate in these ways, it is difficult to develop a sense of emotional well-being. This can limit and constrict a person's ability to connect with others. To a certain extent, the quality of our relationships is based on whether or how we communicate our feelings. However, we can develop communication skills that will allow us to enjoy healthier and more gratifying relationships.

# Between-Sessions Activity

On this page please respond to each of the scale items in terms of how you act now. You assessed yourself on this scale at the beginning of this module and you can compare that to where you are now.

## Recovery Scale: Self

Please take a few moments to mark the degree to which you do each of the following things. Make an "X" or a circle on each line to indicate your response. You will not have to compare your answers with anyone else's, and you will not be judged on how well you are doing. This is not a test, but an opportunity for you to chart your own progress in recovery.

| | Not at All | Just a Little | Pretty Much | Very Much |
|---|---|---|---|---|
| 1. I keep up my physical appearance (bathing, hair, clean clothes, nails). | | | | |
| 2. I exercise regularly. | | | | |
| 3. I eat healthy meals. | | | | |
| 4. I get restful sleep. | | | | |
| 5. I go to work/school (or I complete required tasks). | | | | |
| 6. I can adapt to change. | | | | |
| 7. I keep up my living space. | | | | |
| 8. I take constructive criticism well. | | | | |
| 9. I can accept praise. | | | | |
| 10. I laugh at funny things. | | | | |
| 11. I acknowledge my needs and feelings. | | | | |
| 12. I engage in new interests. | | | | |
| 13. I can relax without alcohol or other drugs. | | | | |
| 14. I value myself. | | | | |

# Reflections on Recovery

In the space below, please write any thoughts, feelings, or questions that you might have about what was covered in this session.

# MODULE B

# Relationships

Because of a myth that men easily live and thrive in solitude and self-sufficiency, many people raised to be men appear to devalue relationships and/or do not have a lot of confidence in their ability to be in successful relationships. However, all people grow (or fail to grow) primarily in relationships.

This second module, Relationships, addresses how our early family relationships influence us, how the different relationships we have over the courses of our lives affect us, and how our relationships either support or harm our recovery. The sessions in this module examine what it takes for a person to create healthy relationships and the barriers that get in the way of healthy relationships. They present some of the skills necessary to create those healthy relationships (including effective communication and conflict resolution) and provide an opportunity for you to practice those skills in the safety of your group.

Remember, when you begin to use this workbook after a group session or on your own, take a minute or two to unwind, relax, and focus on where you are now. Just get settled in the way that feels best for you. Allow yourself to notice how you're breathing and then inhale gently and exhale fully. Repeat the breathing exercise two more times. If you experience difficult feelings during the program, try using one of the grounding activities you are learning in the sessions.

# SESSION 7

# Family of Origin

Every family is a system of interwoven relationships. In healthy families, these relationships are supportive and empowering and they foster personal growth. In unhealthy families, particularly if abuse or addiction is present, the relationships become unsupportive and disempowering and they limit personal growth. Children who grow up in unhealthy or high-stress families are at high risk of developing problems with addiction.

Research suggests that children in high-stress families take on specific roles in order to cope. The four roles are the Hero, the Scapegoat, the Lost Child, and the Mascot. These roles help keep the family system in balance. This session explains how these roles appear in a family.

The goals of this session are

- To understand how our relationships in our families of origin affect the ways in which we approach relationships in the present
- To learn some common patterns in family relationships and how to recognize those patterns in our unique families

If you are working this program alone, it may help to ask someone to read the instructions for these activities to you the first few times you do them.

*A Man's Workbook: Helping Men Recover, A Program for Treating Addiction,* Second Edition.
Stephanie S. Covington, Dan Griffin, and Rick Dauer.
© 2022 Stephanie S. Covington, Dan Griffin, and Rick Dauer. Published 2022 by John Wiley & Sons, Inc.

# Deep Breathing

In times of intense fear or stress, taking control of your breathing is one of the best things to do to ground yourself, calm down, and reduce anxiety or panic.

1. Breathe in through your nose and count to four. One, two, three, four. Keep your tongue placed lightly at the roof of your mouth.
2. Hold your breath. One, two, three, four.
3. Breathe out while counting to four. One, two, three, four.
4. Hold again. One, two, three, four.
5. Do the full breathing cycle three more times.

# Containment

Containment is designed to help you temporarily set aside some of your issues and concerns so that you can focus on what is going on now. It is an effective way to reduce your stress and anxiety and allow you to better deal with the present.

1. In your mind's eye, create a list of all the thoughts and feelings that are bothering you right now. Include any strong negative emotions, thoughts, and memories. For the first couple of times, you can write these down if that is easier for you.
2. Visualize a container of some kind that can hold objects. It can be a box, a trash can, or anything that has a lid you can close. Or it can be a closet with a door that you can close.
3. Imagine depositing each of your worries and concerns and bad memories into the container.
4. Place all the distressing items into the container, knowing that it's just for a brief period of time. You can retrieve any and all of these items at any time.
5. When you have set aside all the things that are upsetting you, bring your attention back to the present and what you want to pay attention to.

# Family Roles

The most influential relationships for most of us are the ones we had as children with the people with whom we grew up. Those relationships established patterns for how we relate to men, women, authority figures, peers, and ourselves. The role a child takes on in the family of origin is one of the major forces that shape who the child becomes. Roles help children to learn how to interact with others and to set boundaries (or not). These roles are not naturally positive or negative. They often are associated with birth order.

Most people with substance use disorders come from families in which their needs were not met. Children in distressed homes often adopt rigidly defined roles in an effort to survive in emotionally empty or challenging environments. They believe that the roles will keep them safe. People in such families often try to bolster their feelings of confusion, lack of safety, and low self-esteem by hiding behind clearly defined and predictable roles, and family members resist role flexibility. For example, in abusive homes, children may try to divert the abuser's attention from other family members in an attempt to keep them safe.

Because they are responses to external cues, rigid roles are not the children's freely chosen expressions of their internal states. And reacting out of a rigid role limits the free range of expression, so the person cannot respond to the unique aspects of a particular situation.

## Four Typical Roles

1. The firstborn child is called the "Hero." The Hero has all the privileges of an only child for a while. When a brother or sister is born, the firstborn may feel threatened at first but then will look for a way to win back the parents' attention and approval. The Hero often will identify with their values and rules and will try to follow all the rules perfectly and to perform in an outstanding manner. The more unstable the parents look, the more the Hero will try to perform perfectly in order to keep the family together. The Hero often gets good grades and excels in activities, becomes super-responsible, and wants to be in control at all times.

2. The second child often becomes the "Scapegoat." Scapegoats get attention at home from acting out. Sometimes they deliberately cause trouble just to escape boredom. As much trouble as this child causes, the Scapegoat relieves stress in the family by taking attention away from the issues between Mom and Dad that aren't being addressed. Everyone can pretend that the family's problem is the

Scapegoat. The Scapegoat may be at risk for physical abuse as punishment from a parent, school official, or anyone in a position of authority. Physical abuse of boys is more accepted as a form of discipline than it is for girls, so a male Scapegoat is a likely target. This child is more sensitive to negative peer pressure than the Hero is and is more likely to skip school, engage in unsafe sex, shoplift, or use alcohol or other drugs. Or the child may withdraw, acting disengaged at home.

3. The thirdborn is called the "Lost Child." This child stays home and reads, sits at a computer, plays video games, watches television, and generally hangs out alone. The Lost Child lives in a world of imagination. In a healthy family, a third child might learn to compete and excel in something different from the others. But in a high-stress family, the child is happy to fade into the background. The Lost Child often is at high risk for sexual abuse and teenage suicide as a result of being isolated and, therefore, vulnerable.

4. In healthy families, the last child, called the "Mascot," is often the most relaxed and cheerful. Parents may have relaxed their child-rearing methods by now, and this child has plenty of opportunity to play with brothers and sisters. But in a troubled home, each additional child adds more stress to the family. Each has more difficulty getting the parents' attention, because of the attention and energy taken by the addicted parent. So, the fourth child often steps into the role of family Mascot and will do anything to attract attention. The Mascot may use humor, charm, or hyperactivity. As much trouble as this can be, it takes the focus off the tension between Mom and Dad and helps to relieve family stress. Like the Scapegoat, the Mascot may be at high risk for physical abuse.

Families are not all the same. Single mothers and single fathers raise children, unmarried parents raise children, same-sex couples raise children, and grandparents raise grandchildren. In blended families, children may have two sets of parents, several grandparents, and many stepsisters and stepbrothers. When one or more family members are incarcerated for extended periods of time, it further complicates some of these relationships.

Remembering your family of origin may raise feelings of anger, fear, and pain. This is especially true if you were abused physically, sexually, or psychologically. Your mind may flash back to times when your parents were fighting, when you were yelled at or hit, or when you cried yourself to sleep. It may be difficult to admit that you are having those feelings. When bad feelings from the past are brought up, you can use the breathing and other grounding techniques you have learned to help you become emotionally centered.

# Positive and Negative Aspects of Roles

## Hero

| Positive | Negative |
| --- | --- |
| independent | fears rejection, confrontation |
| organized | perfectionist, fears failure |
| responsible | procrastinates |
| avoids harmful risk | doesn't get personal needs met |
| powerful and in control | low self-esteem |
| focused, attentive | unable to play |
| loyal | immature "adult-child" |
| generous with praise | inflexible |
| successful | unable to label feelings |
| leader | guilt ridden |
| high achiever | feels inadequate |
| survivor | fears intimacy |
| motivates self and others | unreasonably high expectations |

## Scapegoat

| Positive | Negative |
| --- | --- |
| many friends | chemically dependent |
| adapts easily | irresponsible |
| exciting life | manipulative |
| handles stress well | daredevil |
| traveler | passive aggressive |
| commands attention | rationalizes |
| fun loving | often on the hot seat |
| adventurous | lies, makes up alibis |
| extrovert | lacks close connections |

## Lost Child

| Positive | Negative |
| --- | --- |
| creative, imaginative | lonely, isolated, withdrawn |
| well-developed skills, manual dexterity | lacks social skills |
| well-read | feels invisible, excluded |
| good listener, observer | can be obsessed with self |

| | |
|---|---|
| spiritual | low self-esteem, distorted self-image |
| resou...l | sad, depressed |
| can w rk independently | mistrusts, blames others |
| nonconformist | fantasizes |
| enjoys solitude | inactive, indecisive |

### Mascot

| <u>Positive</u> | <u>Negative</u> |
|---|---|
| sense of humor | never taken seriously |
| charming | blames, projects |
| joyful | denies own feelings to maintain image |
| eases family tension, keeps the peace | dependent |
| playful, active | irresponsible |
| attracts attention | seeks attention |
| | deflects attention from real problem |

Source: *Leaving the Enchanted Forest: The Path from Relationship Addiction to Intimacy,* by Stephanie Covington and Liana Beckett, 1988. San Francisco, CA: HarperSanFrancisco. Copyright 1988 by Stephanie Covington and Liana Beckett. Reprinted with permission of HarperCollins.

# Family Roles: Discussion Questions

Each child has a primary family role. However, you might have had a secondary role that you took on when the primary role didn't work for some reason. For example, maybe you were the Hero until one of your brothers became a sports star and became the Hero, so you took on the role of Scapegoat. If you were sent to a new foster family, you likely had to find a new role.

These family roles were important to our survival as children, but most of us carry them into adulthood, even though they may not be useful in our lives now.

Please consider and answer the following questions.

1. What was your primary role in your family?

2. What positive aspects of your role can you identify?

3. What negative aspects of your role can you identify?

4. As you think about your family role, is there any part of it that you would like to leave behind as you move forward in life? If so, what is it?

5. Which of the positive attributes will be a source of strength for you in recovery?

6. Are there ways that your family role is affecting your current relationships? What do you notice?

# Between-Sessions Activities

1. You also can practice the Containment activity (on page 62) between now and our next session.

## Recovery Scale: Relationships

Please take a few moments to mark the degree to which you do each of the following things. Make an "X" or a circle on each line to indicate your response. You will complete this form again at the end of this module on Relationships to see how you have changed. You will not have to compare your answers with anyone else's, and you will not be judged on how well you are doing. This is not a test, but an opportunity for you to chart your own progress in recovery.

| | Not at All | Just a Little | Pretty Much | Very Much |
|---|---|---|---|---|
| 1. I share my needs and wants with others. | | | | |
| 2. I socialize with others. | | | | |
| 3. I stay connected to friends and loved ones. | | | | |
| 4. I nurture my children and/or loved ones. | | | | |
| 5. I am straightforward with others. | | | | |
| 6. I can tell the difference between supportive and non-supportive relationships. | | | | |
| 7. I have developed a support system. | | | | |
| 8. I offer support to others. | | | | |
| 9. I participate in conversations with my family members, friends, and/or coworkers. | | | | |
| 10. I listen to and respect others. | | | | |
| 11. I have clean and sober friends. | | | | |
| 12. I can be trusted. | | | | |

# Reflections on Recovery

In the space below, please write any thoughts, feelings, or questions that you might have about what was covered in this session.

# Barriers to Healthy Relationships

In the previous session, you learned some of the ways in which interactions among family members can have long-lasting effects on every part of your life. In high-stress families, there is a risk that the children will be abused. If parents use alcohol or other drugs, the risk is higher. Many children do not know that they have been abused because they assume that the behaviors in their families are normal.

This session helps people to consider the attitudes and behaviors that get in the way of having healthy relationships. It includes the issue of control and how excessive control can lead to abuse, and even escalate to violence. It also points out how we can integrate control and power into our lives in healthy ways.

The goals of this session are

- To understand the different forms of abuse
- To learn that people with substance use disorders often have histories of abuse and other forms of trauma
- To understand some of the barriers to healthy relationships
- To consider the effects that power, control, violence, and other forms of abuse have had on the participants' relationships

*A Man's Workbook: Helping Men Recover, A Program for Treating Addiction,* Second Edition.
Stephanie S. Covington, Dan Griffin, and Rick Dauer.
© 2022 Stephanie S. Covington, Dan Griffin, and Rick Dauer. Published 2022 by John Wiley & Sons, Inc.

# Abuse

A lot of violence and abuse stem from humans' desire have power and control over our feelings, our behaviors, other people's feelings and behaviors, our environment, our position in our community, how others see us, and so on. When our efforts to exert control are unsuccessful, we may become frustrated and angry and we may direct these at another person in ways that are emotionally or physically damaging.

Some abuse is linked to issues of attachment, which may result when a child is unable to have a consistent emotional connection with a parent or primary caregiver. Some is linked to issues of self-esteem, self-doubt, and/or shame.

More than one in nine children are exposed to family violence annually in the United States, and one in four children are exposed to family violence in their lifetimes. Much of the violence witnessed is perpetrated by males. Girls and women are more likely to be exposed to psychological and physical intimate partner violence throughout their lifetimes.

It is not uncommon for people to experience multiple kinds of abuse in their lifetimes. Within the United States, approximately 16 percent of men and 25 to 27 percent of women report having experienced childhood sexual abuse; those who experienced sexual abuse also had higher rates of childhood physical abuse, maltreatment, and neglect.

Children who experienced childhood abuse and neglect are significantly more likely as adults to perpetrate criminal violence, abuse their own children, and commit intimate partner violence than are adults without such histories. They may abuse others in an effort to assert their power. If they grew up in troubled or high-stress families, they were not able to learn healthy coping mechanisms with which to manage their frustration and anger. Males who witness family violence or who have experienced trauma have a higher rate of perpetrating violence as adults. There is the saying that "hurt people hurt people."

There is a difference in occurrence of violence with respect to sexual and gender identity. Among individuals who have experienced sexual violence other than rape, 20 percent of heterosexual men have, 40 percent of gay men have, 47 percent of bisexual men have, 17 percent of heterosexual women have, 13 percent of lesbians have, and 46 percent of bisexual women have. Lesbian, gay, bisexual, transgender, and gender nonconforming teenagers experience higher rates of bullying, physical and sexual violence, and drug use than do their heterosexual peers.

Many people who are victims of abuse feel weak, powerless, and shamed. They blame themselves for not being able to prevent the abuse. Alcohol and other drugs are initially effective in managing these distressing feelings; however, the use of chemicals

72

is likely to make them worse them over time. If the abuse resulted in trauma, they may use alcohol and other drugs as an automatic reaction when the trauma is triggered by a related event or memory.

The good news is that we can change these patterns. Also, looking at your own history might help you to address the hurt from your pasts.

## Types of Abuse

Following are examples of types of abuse. In the spaces provided, you may list additional behaviors that you can think of or that are identified during the group discussion.

*Physical Abuse:* Examples of physical abuse are pinching, slapping, pushing, hair pulling, spitting, restraining, shaking, kicking, choking, dragging, ripping clothing, biting, throwing objects, hitting with objects, punching, burning, and stabbing.

*Verbal Abuse:* Examples of verbal abuse are name calling, ridicule, constant criticism, blaming, threatening, and shouting or screaming.

*Emotional Abuse:* Examples of emotional abuse are silence, withdrawing, withholding approval or affection, name calling and using slurs, manipulation through dishonesty, intimidation, not acknowledging the other person's feelings, and calling the other person's feelings "hysterical" or "crazy."

*Sexual Abuse:* Examples of sexual abuse are telling sexual jokes, harassment, violating other's boundaries, giving inappropriate information, inappropriate touching, voyeurism, sexual hugs, commenting about developing bodies, reading or viewing pornography with a child, exhibitionism, fondling, French kissing a child, oral sex, and penetration.

| Sexual Abuse Continuum | | |
|---|---|---|
| **Psychological Abuse** | **Covert Abuse** | **Overt Abuse** |
| Sexual jokes | "Inadvertent" inappropriate touching | Exhibitionism |
| Verbal harassment | Household voyeurism | Fondling |
| Violating boundaries | Ridicule of developing bodies | French kissing |
| Telling children inappropriate sexual information | Sexual hugs | Oral sex |
| | Pornographic reading or video watching with child | Penetration |

Some lasting effects of abuse are powerlessness, numbness, rage, hatred, shame, fear, mistrust, confusion, poor self-esteem, poor judgment, antisocial behavior, fear of intimacy, over-sexualized behavior, and an inability to have healthy sexual relationships. In addition, children raised in abusive homes are at high risk to become addicted to alcohol and other drugs, and people who are victims of abuse are at risk of becoming abusers.

Acknowledging abuse can be difficult for people if they associate it with admitting weakness. As a result, many people keep their histories of abuse hidden, from themselves as well as others, in order to feel strong and in control of their lives. It is important to know that, if you were abused as a child, it was wrong and it was not your fault. No matter what you did or what you were told, it was inexcusable.

# Trauma

The Substance Abuse and Mental Health Services Administration defines trauma as "an event, series of events, or set of circumstances that is experienced by an individual as physically or emotionally harmful or life threatening and that has lasting adverse effects on the individual's functioning and mental, physical, social, emotional, or spiritual well-being." A simpler way to understand trauma is that it happens when an external threat overwhelms a person's normal physical and psychological coping mechanisms. It is important to understand that trauma is both an event and an individual's response to the event. What is traumatic for one person may not be traumatic for another.

One possible result of trauma is posttraumatic stress disorder. The American Psychiatric Association lists the symptoms of PTSD as

- Reexperiencing the event through nightmares and flashbacks
- Avoidance of stimuli associated with the event. For example, if a child was sexually assaulted by a blonde babysitter, the child may have problems with blonde women, especially babysitters.
- Estrangement (the inability to be emotionally close to anyone)
- Numbing of general responsiveness (feeling nothing most of the time)
- Hypervigilance (constantly scanning one's environment for danger, whether physical or emotional)
- An exaggerated startle response (a tendency to jump at loud noises or unexpected touch)

If you have been traumatized, you may recognize some of these symptoms. Unresolved trauma can affect your physical health, your emotional well-being, your ability to develop and maintain healthy relationships, and your sexual health. You may be comforted to know that there is a name for what you are experiencing, that you are not alone, and that there are people who understand and can help. Part of the process of healing from trauma, like recovering from addiction, is developing connection and support with others.

# A Place of Peace Visualization

1. Close your eyes or lower your eyelids.

2. Take a deep breath in while you silently count to four. One, two, three, four.

3. Now breathe out slowly. One, two, three, four.

4. Breathe from your abdomen. Breathe in again. One, two, three, four.

5. And out again. One, two, three, four.

6. Now picture in your mind a place of peace. Maybe you have been there before or, maybe it is a place of your dreams. Maybe it's your bed or a comfortable chair. Maybe it's sitting by a lake or lying in the sun at the ocean. Maybe it's a special place you visited as a child or a scene from one of your favorite movies. It may be a real place or an imaginary place. See that place in your mind.

7. Keep breathing slowly and deeply.

8. Let the muscles in your face relax.

9. Repeat the breathing process two more times.

10. Let your brow relax.

11. Let your jaw relax.

12. Let your neck and your shoulders relax. Imagine all the tension draining out of them. Let it go.

13. Let your hands and arms go limp next to you.

14. Let your middle relax—your chest and your abdomen.

15. Keep breathing in and out.

16. Let your hips and your legs relax.

17. Let your feet relax.

18. Relax your whole body and imagine yourself in that favorite, safe place. This is your place of safety and peace. Your life is the way you always wanted it to be. You are sober. You are loving and caring and committed to being of service to others.

19. Your life is full of peace. You are full of peace.

20. As you breathe in these next couple of times, breathe in the word "peace."

21. As you breathe out, exhale all the pain from your past and all the negative feelings and thoughts.

22. Breathe in peace.

23. Breathe out pain.

24. Now open your eyes and slowly return to the present.

# The Power and Control Wheel

In our society, men tend to have more power than women and children. Some people use that power in abusive ways to control situations and other people. Correctional facilities frequently use power and control, sometimes in abusive ways, to maintain security and safety.

The figure that follows is the Power and Control Wheel. Each segment or spoke of the wheel represent ways that one person can be abusive to another.

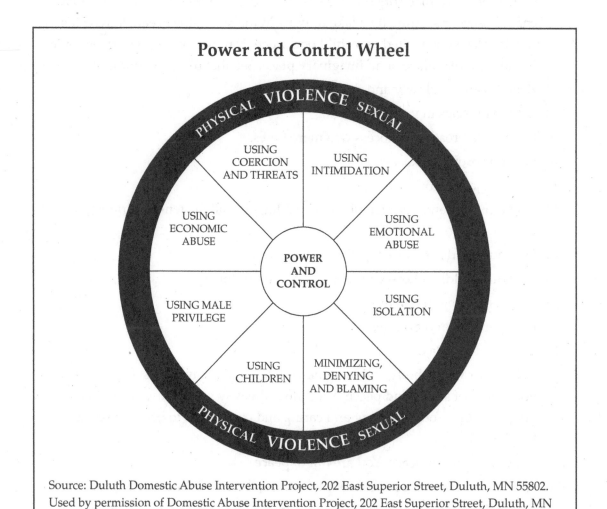

**Power and Control Wheel**

Source: Duluth Domestic Abuse Intervention Project, 202 East Superior Street, Duluth, MN 55802. Used by permission of Domestic Abuse Intervention Project, 202 East Superior Street, Duluth, MN 55802. 212-722-2781. www.duluth-model.org.

The twelve types of abuse that are part of the Power and Control Wheel are

1. Emotional abuse
2. Physical abuse
3. Economic abuse
4. Sexual abuse
5. Coercion and threats
6. Intimidation
7. Isolation
8. Using children
9. Using male privilege
10. Minimizing
11. Denying
12. Blaming

Interpersonal violence is defined as: "the intentional use of physical force or power, threatened or actual, against a person or group that results in or has a high likelihood of resulting in injury, death psychological harm, maldevelopment, or deprivation."

The important factors are the behaviors that either threaten or abuse people, and the intentions or motives: to harm or exert power. Some degree of abusiveness seems to be tolerated in some people's concept of masculinity. You may have acted abusively or violently because you were overwhelmed with emotion or acting out of a traumatic trigger. Sometimes these behaviors have become such a part of how we interact with others that we don't even realize why we are doing them. So we may not understand how inappropriate and unacceptable these behaviors are. Abusive behavior is damaging to both the victim and the perpetrator. It is never appropriate or justifiable.

Power and control are not necessarily bad; it is just that the tactics that a lot of us use can be harmful to ourselves and others.

Ask yourself these questions regarding how you treat others:

• Is the behavior getting you what you want?

- Does it reflect the person you want to be?

- How would you like it if you were treated that way?

# Between-Sessions Activity

Between now and the next session, use the space provided to answer these two questions:

1. What are some examples of how we can use our personal power in positive ways?

2. Can you provide any examples from your recovery where you have already begun to use power in a constructive way?

# Reflections on Recovery

In the space below, please write any thoughts, feelings, or questions that you might have about what was covered in this session.

# SESSION 9

# Fathers

This session focuses on fathers or father figures. A father—whether or not he was present in a young person's life—is a primary role model. Addiction, abuse, and other problematic behaviors often are generational. The father-child relationship is crucial to the child's sense of self and what the child thinks it means to be a man. Many of us have had fathers who were emotionally and/or physically absent from our lives.

However, your father has probably had more influence on you than you may realize. Even those who have never met their biological fathers probably have developed psychological and emotional relationships with their fathers in their minds.

It can be hard for children to think of their fathers and mothers as people. However, the roles of father and mother can be challenging and limiting. As an adult, when you begin to see your parents as human, you can begin to deal with your feelings about them.

Understanding your father as a person can help you to appreciate your own masculinity. For example, if you are angry with your father, you may tend to have conflict with other men, especially those who remind you of your father. Or you may have a hard time trusting them as a result of how your father treated you when you were a child.

*A Man's Workbook: Helping Men Recover, A Program for Treating Addiction,* Second Edition.
Stephanie S. Covington, Dan Griffin, and Rick Dauer.
© 2022 Stephanie S. Covington, Dan Griffin, and Rick Dauer. Published 2022 by John Wiley & Sons, Inc.

The goals of this session are

- To begin to explore our relationships with our fathers or father substitutes
- To begin to consider our fathers as individual men
- To begin a discussion of our experiences as children of our fathers
- To recognize the roles our fathers played in shaping who we are today

# Fathers

Most of you have had some kind of father figure in your lives, even if you were not raised by your biological father. It may have been a grandfather, uncle, adoptive father, foster father, your mother's partner, or someone else. You may have felt close to your biological father or the person who fulfilled this role or you may have felt distant from him. You may have felt many emotions about him, including love, pride, anger, resentment, and sadness. Maybe your emotions have changed as you have grown up. No matter what our fathers did or did not do, we often have strong feelings about them. Even as adults, we often still carry feelings about what we wish our fathers were like and how we wish our relationships with them could have been.

The influence of a father or father substitute plays a large part in a person's development and attitudes about men. You may have grown up committed to *not* being like your father because of the pain involved in that relationship. You may blame your father for what he did or did not do. You may have looked up to your father, your hero, and wanted to be like him. This kind of father probably protected you and provided for you. Maybe he taught you about love and compassion as much as he taught you about being a provider and a fighter. Or maybe your relationship with your father was somewhere in between. There are so many different ways that fathers show up in our lives, and all of them play a critical role in shaping the people that we become.

# Our Father's Lives: Discussion Questions

1. What do you know about your father's life when he was a child? How about when he was a teenager? An adult?

2. To your knowledge, was your dad ever rebellious or unhappy in his role as a man and husband? What did he do about it?

3. Do you believe that your father was able to achieve the goals he had set for himself? What were some of these?

4. Did your father have a problem with alcohol or other drugs? If so, discuss some specific ways in which you were affected by this.

5. Did your father ever get in trouble with the legal system? If so, how did this affect you and the rest of your family?

6. What did you learn about being a man from your father?

# Fathers and Children: Discussion Questions

1. Think back to when you were a child under the age of twelve. What was your relationship with your father—or the person who was substituting in the role of your father—like at that time?

2. What was your relationship with your father or father substitute like when you were a teenager?

3. How would you describe your current relationship with him? If your father is no longer alive, how would you describe the way you think about and remember him?

4. In what ways do you think that your father is, or would be, disappointed in the person that you have become?

5. In what ways do you think that your father is, or would be, proud of the person you have become?

6. If there is something left unsaid in your relationship with your father, whether he is still alive or not, what is it?

One of the goals of these activities is to help you to see your father as a human being, with his own dreams, challenges, disappointments, and successes and to help you to let go of some of the expectations and the pain.

# Breathing and Visualization

As you breathe in during this exercise, imagine all the peaceful and joyful times you had with your father. As you breathe out, breathe out any of the pain you feel regarding your father, particularly any of the feelings or memories that came up in the session.

1. Slowly, take in a deep breath.
2. Now let it out.
3. Breathe in again slowly. Think of all the good times you have had with your father. You may even want to smile.
4. Now, breathe out slowly. Release any pain you carry from your relationship with your father. You may want to make a sound as you release it.
5. Repeat this. Breathe in slowly. Remember the good times you have had with your father.
6. Breathe out slowly. Release any pain you carry from your relationship with your father.
7. Breathe in.
8. Breathe out.
9. Breathe in.
10. Breathe out.

# Between-Sessions Activity

Between now and the next session, you will write a letter to your father. You won't necessarily mail this letter and you don't have to share it with him at all, but it will be an opportunity for you to acknowledge and express your thoughts and feelings. You may choose to write some things that you have never been able to say to him. If your biological father was not present when you were growing up, you may still have some powerful feelings that you would like to share. Or, you could write a letter to another adult male figure in your life, such as an uncle, grandfather, or even an older brother. If you had a father and a stepfather, you can decide which one you want to write to.

Spelling and grammar don't matter; just write what is in your heart. Try to be as honest as possible in identifying both positive and negative emotions.

Writing will probably be easiest for you, but if you prefer, some other means of communication is fine. You may write an original song or rap, write a poem, play a musical piece, draw a picture, do a drawing, or utilize some other form of creative expression that represents what you want to say to your father. If English is not your first language, you may write your letter in whatever language you are most fluent in.

You can use the space provided on the following page to write or draw your message to your father. If you prefer, or if you need more space, do your writing or drawing on a separate piece of paper.

You will be invited to share your "letter" during the next session. If you are not comfortable sharing with your group members, you may be asked to explain why. Even if you are planning not to share, please complete the assignment.

If you are using this workbook individually, complete your communication with your "father" and then make some notes about how you felt when you reviewed it. If you can, you may want to share what this activity brings up for you with a counselor, therapist, or trusted friend.

Dear

# Reflections on Recovery

In the space below, please write any thoughts, feelings, or questions that you might have about what was covered in this session.

# Mothers

Regardless of the relationship you had with your father, your mother may have been more constant in your life. Despite significant changes in our society, mothers continue to do the majority of the child rearing in most families. That is what mothers are expected to do. You may have been taught what to *think* about your feelings by your father, but your mother showed you what it is like to be cared for, so she helped you to *experience* feelings. At least, that's what we expect of mothers. However, for a variety of reasons, not all mothers are able to live up to our expectations.

The intrinsic value of child rearing historically has been taken for granted or downplayed by people who did not have to do it. Some of you may have seen this reflected in the ways your fathers or other men treated your mothers. How your father or the other men in your life treated your mother, and how you may have perceived your mother allowing herself to be treated, affected how you thought of your mother. More to the point, it affects how you think of women in general and how you treat women.

The goals of this session are

- To begin to explore our relationships with our mothers or mother substitutes
- To begin to consider our mothers as individual women
- To recognize the roles our mothers played in shaping who we are today
- To understand the connections between our relationships with our mothers and how we treat women today

*A Man's Workbook: Helping Men Recover, A Program for Treating Addiction,* Second Edition.
Stephanie S. Covington, Dan Griffin, and Rick Dauer.
© 2022 Stephanie S. Covington, Dan Griffin, and Rick Dauer. Published 2022 by John Wiley & Sons, Inc.

# On Being a Father: Discussion Questions

This session wraps up the discussion of fathers. Not everybody who uses this workbook is a father. If that is the case, you can choose to pass on this activity, or you can imagine what your responses to the questions might be, or imagine how *your* father would answer the questions.

1. If you are a father, what did you expect to feel when you had children? What did you actually feel?

2. Did you have an idea of how you wanted to be as a father? How hard has it been to be the father you wanted to be?

3. For those of you who do not have children, what did you hear in this discussion that you think might be helpful for you in the future?

# Mothers and Children: Discussion Questions

Mothers traditionally have been the nurturers, because The Woman Rules tell girls and women that taking care of others' needs is the primary role of women. Your mother is supposed to be the one who is there for you. The best moms show up when we need them. They love and nurture us and teach us about ourselves. At least, that's what we expect them to do. Of course, we know that it doesn't work out that way for everybody. But it is how our society thinks of mothers. It is a pressure that we put on mothers and that some of them put on themselves.

However, not all moms can live up to that ideal. They are human, and we have to allow them to be human. Nobody is perfect. Some mothers are unable to meet even the basic expectations of parenting, so it is our fathers or other family members or foster parents who become our primary caregivers.

Our society does not always do a good job of helping mothers. The essential value of child rearing historically has been taken for granted or downplayed by people who did not have to do it. Some of you may have seen this reflected in the ways your fathers or other men treated and devalued your mothers.

Even if some of you were raised solely by your mother (or mother substitute), there may be some ambivalence in your feelings about her. It is also important to understand that the mother may have been the abusive and/or addicted parent in the family. Also, a lot of people feel anger toward their mothers—although it may be deep below the surface—for failing to protect them from abusive fathers, older siblings, or other adult males.

1. Think back to when you were a child under the age of twelve. What was your relationship with your mother—or the person who played the role of your mother—like at that time?

2. What was your relationship with your mother like when you were a teenager?

3. How would you describe your relationship with her now? If your mother is no longer alive, how would you describe how you think and feel about your memories of her?

4. Did your mother ever have a problem with alcohol or other drugs? If so, discuss some specific ways in which you were affected by this.

5. Did your mother ever have any difficulties with the legal system? If so, what was that like for you?

6. How did your father or other men treat your mother?

Understanding our mothers as real women can help us to better understand how we relate to and treat other women in our lives. It also can help us to honor the parts of us that often are described as "feminine": our sensitivity, compassion, creativity, gentleness, and caring for others. If we are angry with our mothers, we may tend to treat women badly, especially those who remind us of our mothers.

# Breathing and Visualization

This brief grounding activity is similar to the one in the last session. You'll be slowly taking in a deep breath and then letting it out. As you draw your breath in, imagine all the peaceful and joyful times you had with your mother or mother substitute. As you breathe out, breathe out any of the pain you feel about your mother, particularly any of the feelings or memories that came up today.

You will do this four times.

1. Breathe in slowly. Envision the good times you've had with your mother. You may even want to smile.
2. Now, breathe out slowly. Release any pain you carry from your relationship with your mother. You may want to make a sound as you release it.
3. Repeat this. Breathe in.
4. Breathe out and release.

# Between-Sessions Activity

Your assignment, to be completed between now and the next session, is to write a letter to your mother. You won't necessarily mail this letter and you don't have to share it with her at all, but it will be an opportunity for you to acknowledge and express your thoughts and feelings. You may choose to write down some things that you have never been able to say to her. If your biological mother was not present when you were growing up, you may still have some powerful feelings that you would like to share. Or, you could write a letter to another adult female figure in your life such as an aunt, grandmother, or even an older sister. If you had a mother and a stepmother, you can decide which one you want to write to.

Spelling and grammar don't matter; just write what is in your heart. If English is not your first language, you may write your letter in whatever language you are most fluent in. Try to be as honest as possible in identifying both positive and negative emotions.

Writing will probably be easiest for you, but if you prefer, alternate means of communication are encouraged. You may write a song or rap, play a musical piece, draw, or utilize some other form of creative expression.

You will be invited to share your "letter" during our next session. If you are not comfortable sharing with your group members, we will honor that, but we would expect that you would briefly explain why. Even if you are planning not to share, we still ask that you complete the assignment. You can use the space provided on the following page to write or draw your message to your mother. If you prefer, or if you need more space, do your writing or drawing on a separate piece of paper.

If you are using this workbook individually, complete your communication with your "mother" and then make some notes about how you felt when you reviewed it. If you can, you may want to share what this activity brings up for you with a counselor, therapist, or trusted friend.

Dear

# Reflections on Recovery

In the space below, please write any thoughts, feelings, or questions that you might have about what was covered in this session.

# Creating Healthy Relationships and Support Systems

This session explores how critical it is for a person in recovery to develop and maintain supportive, growth-fostering relationships. The previous two sessions emphasized your relationships with your mother and father, because these are probably the ones that have had the greatest influence in your life. However, other relationships are extremely important, including those with your spouse or partner, your friends, your , your co-workers, and so on. Some of your relationships undoubtedly have been healthy and supportive, and some probably have been unhealthy and unsupportive.

Addiction is a downward spiral and, as your addiction takes over your life, your relationships follow you down in that spiral. You push away the healthier people in your life or they leave. The relationships that are associated with addiction tend to be problematic. You are not likely to grow in those relationships, and they are never as important as the addiction.

Recovery is growth. It is an upward spiral in which your life is expanding. In recovery, we begin to form healthier relationships. We move from isolation to connections and community. A supportive relationship should help you to grow. A supportive relationship gives you energy, helps you to believe in yourself, and encourages you to pursue your goals.

*A Man's Workbook: Helping Men Recover, A Program for Treating Addiction*, Second Edition.
Stephanie S. Covington, Dan Griffin, and Rick Dauer.
© 2022 Stephanie S. Covington, Dan Griffin, and Rick Dauer. Published 2022 by John Wiley & Sons, Inc.

The goals of this session are

- To understand the importance of supportive, growth-fostering relationships
- To assess the supportiveness of our current relationships
- To begin developing sober support systems

# Grounding Activity

The following grounding activity is designed to help you with any feelings that the letter writing and sharing may have brought up.

1. Take a deep breath in through your nose. Let it out through your mouth.
2. Take another deep breath in through your nose, hold it, and let it out through your mouth with a sigh.
3. Now, breathe in any of the positive thoughts and experiences you have about your mother.
4. Breathe out any of the pain and negativity.
5. Do that two more times.

# Supportive, Growth-Fostering Relationships

Supportive relationships help us grow. They provide us with energy, empowerment, and knowledge. They help us to believe in ourselves and contribute to our feelings of self-worth. They encourage us to pursue our goals. They provide healthy connections.

Support can include lots of things. Emotional support when you're going through a hard time can be as simple as someone really listening to you without giving advice and trying to fix you. You might consider practicing this kind of support by telling your sponsor or a friend, "I want to talk about something and I am not looking for feedback; I would just like to be heard." Practical support can be having someone help you do one of the Between-Sessions Activities. Someone might support your recovery by checking in with you every day to see how you're doing and patting you on the back because you've had another day without alcohol or other drugs.

# Discussion Questions

1. You've been in this program for up to eleven sessions now. What are some ways in which you've felt supported here?

2. Of the various kinds of support that you've had in your life, which have been especially helpful?

3. What are some of the reasons that you find it difficult to ask for support?

4. Can you think of a time in your life when you were in crisis or having a hard time and you enlisted the support of someone else? What was that like?

# Boundaries

We have stressed how important it is to develop and maintain healthy relationships. You may have interpreted that to mean that you need to end every relationship with people who use alcohol or other drugs. This is not necessarily so. However, you do need to learn how to set boundaries with people.

Boundaries are guidelines we create to establish how we expect to be treated by others. They provide limits on what others can and can't do, and they provide limits on what we are willing to do or not do. There are physical, sexual, emotional, and relational boundaries.

We adapt our boundaries based on the situation and the other people involved. Flexible boundaries are firm and clear, although they can evolve over time and can be adjusted according to new developments or information.

It takes practice to learn how to set and maintain healthy boundaries that protect you in respectful ways but also let you have close, healthy relationships with others. You don't have to be angry, mean, hostile, abusive, or rigid when setting boundaries. You can be respectful and kind while also being assertive and firm.

You need to be very direct with people about the boundaries you have established for yourself. These dictate that sobriety is the highest priority in your life. When you enforce your rules, some of your family members, or friends, or even your partner may not respect your wishes. When your friends and family members do respect them, you will know that there is more to the relationship than just using together, and that becomes something to build on.

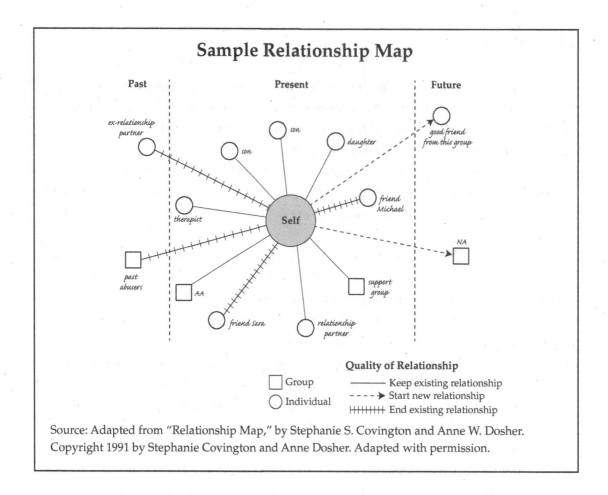

**Sample Relationship Map**

Source: Adapted from "Relationship Map," by Stephanie S. Covington and Anne W. Dosher. Copyright 1991 by Stephanie Covington and Anne Dosher. Adapted with permission.

# Relationship Maps

The illustration above is an example of what a Relationship Map might look like. It shows one person's relationships to people in the past and present, as well as plans for the future. You will create your own map using the diagram on page 111. You can see that you will put yourself in the middle of the page in a circle. Then you add the other relationships in your life. You draw circles for individuals and squares for groups.

Perhaps each of your parents, your friend, your significant other, and each of your children is in a circle as a present relationship. Your ex-partner is entered as a past relationship. Your group in this program is a present relationship in a square because it's a group. If you are in A.A., C.A., or N.A. now, put those groups in squares in the present. If you are not yet going to Twelve Step or other mutual support meetings, you might put a square for them in the future section of your map if that's a source of support you want to add.

*Helping Men Recover A Man's Workbook*

Then notice the different kinds of lines that connect the self to the other individuals and groups. A solid line shows that this is a relationship you already have that you want to maintain. A dotted line with an arrow toward the other person is a relationship that you want to start. Maybe you are not already going to A.A. but want to start. You can't wait around for A.A. to come to you; you have to start that relationship yourself. So, there's a dotted line with an arrow. Last, the solid line with slash marks through it shows that this is a relationship you want to end. Maybe your best friends currently are all alcoholics or drug addicts. They've been drinking or using buddies, but they aren't going to be good support for you in recovery, so maybe you'll decide that you want to end those relationships. Or another possibility: Maybe you'll decide that a particular friend is important enough that you want to keep the relationship, but you need to make some important changes with new boundaries. In that case, the individual should be represented in the past as a relationship that needs to end, and represented in the future as a new type of relationship that you would like to develop.

## Questions To Consider

1. As you look to the future, which of your current relationships do you want to continue and strengthen?

2. Which of your current relationships do you need to end because they will not support your recovery and help you grow?

3. What new, supportive relationships do you want to pursue?

4. You have relationships not just with your family and friends, but also with the community in which you live. What kind of changes in your community would you like to work toward in the future? Identify one step you could take that would begin to make a difference.

# Relationship Map

| Past | Present | Future |
|------|---------|--------|

Self

**Quality of Relationship**

☐ Group

○ Individual

——— Keep existing relationship

- - - → Start new relationship

╟╫╫╫╫╢ End existing relationship

Source: Adapted from "Relationship Map," by Stephanie S. Covington and Anne W. Dosher. Copyright 1991 by Stephanie Covington and Anne Dosher. Adapted with permission.

# Twelve Step Meetings

Twelve Step meetings, such as those presented by Alcoholics Anonymous, Narcotics Anonymous, and Gamblers Anonymous, are places where you can begin to develop supportive relationships. What is great about those meetings is that you are expected to connect with others, get support, and be "a part of." You will not be teased or put down for admitting that you need help, feel scared and confused, or are simply struggling in your addiction. It will be much easier for you to stay in recovery when you are in a culture that embraces, encourages, and even expects supportive relationships.

# Between-Sessions Activity

Your assignment is to continue working on your Relationship Map and the questions on pages 109 and 110. Bring these, as complete as possible, to the next session. You will have the opportunity to share your map with the group.

If you are using this workbook individually, it is still important to complete your Relationship Map and the questions to consider carefully what the implications of these are for you.

# Reflections on Recovery

In the space below, please write any thoughts, feelings, or questions that you might have about what was covered in this session.

# Effective Communication

All humans have basic wants and needs in relationships. We want to be understood, appreciated, cared for, and supported. We need compassion, empathy, affection, physical contact, and cooperation. Asking for these things from your family members, friends, partners, and co-workers is not always easy. As you grew up, you may not have learned how to effectively communicate these wants and needs.

Furthermore, conflict is an inevitable part of any human relationship. No two people are going to agree on everything all the time. How you handle conflict has a large effect on the quality of your relationships.

The goals of this session are

- To evaluate our existing relationships
- To understand and accept that conflict is a natural and even healthy component of relationships
- To learn skills relating to effective communication and conflict resolution

*A Man's Workbook: Helping Men Recover, A Program for Treating Addiction,* Second Edition.
Stephanie S. Covington, Dan Griffin, and Rick Dauer.
© 2022 Stephanie S. Covington, Dan Griffin, and Rick Dauer. Published 2022 by John Wiley & Sons, Inc.

# Sharing Relationship Maps

By now you have completed and (if you are in a group program) shared your Relationship Map. Here are some questions to consider about your map:

- What is your current support system?
- Who will support you in recovery once this program ends?
- Is there any way you can get support from members of this group after this program ends? How could you go about making that happen?
- In what ways do you need to disconnect from your past?
- Are you aware of the need to disconnect from specific people?
- If your friends are using, do you think they're going to be able to support your being clean and sober?
- Are you thinking about joining a Twelve Step or other mutual support group?

You may have more possibilities for receiving support than you had realized before. You don't have to settle for relationships that don't support you. It may be a new concept to think about what you need and want in a relationship. Many of us settle for unhealthy relationships because that is what we know from growing up or because we think that is all we are worth. This mapping activity can help you to evaluate your relationships and explore some of the options available to you. Recovery gives us the opportunity to reinvent ourselves. We get to choose how we want to be and how we want to move through life.

# Communication Styles

There are four basic communication styles. They are:

1. *Passive*. A passive response to a situation is essentially to do nothing or to agree to do something that you really don't want to do. You may believe that you are being treated unfairly yet choose not to say anything. You may see something happening that is wrong and do nothing. Passive behavior is a problematic form of communication because there is no "self" in it. Passive communicators seek to avoid conflict at all costs. We give up our wants and needs in order to temporarily keep the peace.

2. *Passive-Aggressive*. A passive-aggressive response is often the most confusing form of communication. We verbally agree with a request or an opinion in order to avoid conflict and then walk away with the intent of doing something else entirely. An example is agreeing to help a peer complete a job or task, even if you don't want to. Then you show up late, convey a negative attitude, do the work poorly, don't show up at all, and/or complain about the other person later.

3. *Aggressive*. This can be a dangerous form of communication. There is too much "self" in this style. Aggressive communicators want to be "right" and get their way at all costs. Aggressiveness can take the form of yelling, interrupting, blaming, threatening, and even violence. Aggression is often rewarded in the short term, because other people become afraid and back down. We get what we want in the moment, but there is a considerable cost to the relationship. For some of us, what is behind aggressive communication is fear. We may fear loss of control or dominance over the other person or situation. The key is to always feel the real feeling that is there and not let it go into the Anger Funnel unaware.

4. *Assertive*. This form of communication is our goal. When we practice assertiveness, we are clearly stating what we want and need. Assertive communicators respect their own needs and boundaries and those of others. This form of communication is the least emotion driven and most effective in the long term.

It is not unusual, especially in stressful situations, to confuse aggressive and assertive behavior. When we are assertive, we don't blame and we ask for what we want rather than demanding it. We don't make threats or try to intimidate others. We take responsibility for our own feelings.

# Conflict and Communication

A lot of communication in relationships is related to conflict: avoiding, addressing, and resolving it. Although conflict is a normal component of every relationship, most of us are not taught healthy ways of dealing with it. We may have grown up in families in which conflict was avoided at all costs and important issues were left unresolved. Or we may have been raised in environments in which conflict was frequently associated with anger, rage, and even violence. Think about the conflict and threat of conflict you experience every day.

Most of us don't know how to engage in assertive, direct, healthy, and respectful conflict. We may be so afraid of being rejected or being controlled that we overreact to situations and unwittingly create conflict. We may sabotage the relationships that are causing the fear of conflict. Or, because we lack the skills to navigate difficulties, we may abandon the challenges of nurturing a relationship and walk away from people who care about us and whom we care about.

When we are seeking power and control and are in disagreement with others, we may resort to aggression, intimidation, threats, and violence. This leads to problems in our relationships. Sometimes, it leads to more serious consequences, such as physical harm and legal problems. Add alcohol and other drugs to the mix, and a person's behavior is more unpredictable and has the potential to spin out of control. One way to continue making progress in recovery and avoid returning to old behaviors is to learn how to deal effectively with disagreement and conflict.

Here are some things to think about:

1. How many times have you found yourself getting into an argument or a fight with someone when it was the last thing that you wanted to happen?
2. How many arguments have you avoided with someone because you did not want to upset the person?
3. Have you ever talked about other people behind their backs or tried to hurt them in another way without their knowledge?

Nobody is a perfect communicator. Everybody makes mistakes. But when we are aware that we have choices in how we respond to situations and interact with people—that we have behavioral options—we can stop to think and try to communicate more effectively. This will help to strengthen our relationships.

# Scenarios for Group Skits

1. You have made plans to go to a ballgame with your two best friends and already have purchased the tickets. You informed your partner about these plans several weeks ago and you are eagerly looking forward to the day. It is the night before the game, and your partner tells you that family members have been invited over for a cookout and are counting on you being present. Your partner says that you never mentioned your plans and asks you to cancel your plans with your friends.

2. You are living in a halfway house. Your phone is missing. You suspect that it may have been taken by a peer with whom you have had previous conflict. You decide to talk to that person.

3. You have been working at a new job for six months. It is your understanding that you should be reviewed for the possibility of a raise at that point. But your boss has said nothing to you about it. You decide to approach your boss.

# Advantages and Disadvantages of Each Communication Style

Each style of communication and conflict resolution has some advantages and some disadvantages. List as many as you can think of in the spaces that follow.

## Passive

Advantages                                                    Disadvantages

## Passive-Aggressive

Advantages                                                    Disadvantages

# Aggressive

<u>Advantages</u>                                    <u>Disadvantages</u>

# Assertive

<u>Advantages</u>                                    <u>Disadvantages</u>

# Between-Sessions Activity

Between now and the next session, in the space below, describe a recent situation that required conflict resolution. Explain how you handled the conflict. Which style did you use? What was the outcome? Would you do anything differently knowing what you know now?

# Reflections on Recovery

In the space below, please write any thoughts, feelings, or questions that you might have about what was covered in this session.

# Creating and Maintaining Intimacy

When we hear the word "intimacy," many of us immediately think about sex. However, intimacy is an emotional experience of connection with another person that may or may not include sexual activity. Here are some additional definitions of intimacy:

- An expression of feelings in an atmosphere of little or no threat
- Teaching you about me while I'm also learning about you
- Sharing thoughts and feelings with each other in a respectful way—each of us being open and vulnerable
- Love, mutuality, and compassion built on a foundation of respect

You cannot have a healthy, supportive relationship without sharing the "inside of your house." When we accept our inner selves, we can welcome others into our lives. Acknowledging and expressing our feelings fosters intimacy.

Unfortunately, many men allow themselves to express affection and support for one another while engaging in sports because it is considered a "manly" pursuit, but if a friend loses someone he cares for or is going through another difficult experience, it is hard for many men to express sympathy, caring, and affection. This applies to their relationships with intimate partners, as well.

*A Man's Workbook: Helping Men Recover, A Program for Treating Addiction*, Second Edition.
Stephanie S. Covington, Dan Griffin, and Rick Dauer.
© 2022 Stephanie S. Covington, Dan Griffin, and Rick Dauer. Published 2022 by John Wiley & Sons, Inc.

If you are in a relationship, and it feels as if there is no intimacy, the first question to ask is, "Do I feel safe in this relationship?" The second important question is to ask the other person, "Do you feel safe in this relationship?"

The goals of this session are

- To understand the challenges of intimacy
- To recognize how The Man Rules affect the ways in which we conduct adult relationships
- To learn a new assertive communication skill

# Intimacy, Connection, and The Man Rules

All healthy relationships experience a continuous process of connection, disconnection, and reconnection. The true power in relationships comes through reconnection. We could even say that the process of reconnection is a fundamental component of intimacy. Unfortunately, most of us have not been taught the value of reconnection or how to accomplish this. Many of the conflicts and disconnections that arise in our adult relationships are related to what we learned in our families of origin, such as what to value, how to express love, and how to share our feelings and be vulnerable. For example, children raised as girls are taught The Woman Rules, many of which are very different from The Man Rules. Recognizing that both parties in a conflict may be looking at the situation from completely different perspectives helps us in the process of reconnection.

Think back to The Man Rules. Many of those rules—such as don't be emotional, don't ask for help, don't be weak, and always win—keep us from having healthy and fulfilling relationships. They are about disconnection. When our partners and our children ask us to "open up," "share ourselves," and "be supportive," not only do most of us not know what to do, it also scares the heck out of us. Thus, both partners end up frustrated, and we may even end up questioning whether we can successfully be in relationships.

We are engaged in a process of challenging and revising the rules to fit our lives better. We have learned new things about what it means to be connected to others. Recovery teaches us the value of making amends and having difficult and vulnerable conversations.

# Intimacy: Discussion Questions

1. What did intimacy look like in the house where you grew up?

2. What did you learn about intimacy as a teenager?

3. What Man Rule do you struggle with the most in your intimate relationships?

4. Have there been times in the past when you have confused sex and intimacy? Explain what happened.

# The COTE Method of Communication

One common mistake we make that interferes with effective communication and conflict resolution is to blame others for how we feel. How many times have we said "You make me so angry" or "Your behavior really hurt me"? In fact, no one can make us angry or sad or even happy. Our emotions are a function of how we are thinking about a particular occurrence. We tend to think that an event in the external world causes us to feel a certain way. But there is a step in between the event and our emotional response, and that step is the thought we have about the external event. We create a story about what is happening that may or may not be accurate.

When we take responsibility for our own feelings, rather than blaming others, we can expect several immediate benefits. First is that we become personally empowered to make positive change. We are not reliant on others to make us happy; we are taking steps toward creating our own happiness. Our emotions are not subject to decisions or actions taken by another. A second important benefit is that, by not blaming others, we open the door for productive conversation. The others will likely be less defensive and more open to what we have to say. We are more likely to be heard and to have our needs met.

The COTE communication skill is designed to help us be more honest and assertive in our relationships, particularly if there is conflict that needs to be resolved. The basic format is to seek consent, state an observation, describe how you interpreted it, and then own the feeling.

| | |
|---|---|
| Consent | Asking for permission to share difficult thoughts and feelings |
| Observation | Clearly stating what the issue is, without assigning blame |
| Thought | Sharing how we are interpreting what we observe |
| Emotion | Sharing how we feel about the situation |

You might want to practice using this method with a trusted friend or advisor.

# Between-Sessions Activity

## Recovery Scale: Relationships

Please take a few moments to mark the degree to which you do each of the following things. Make an "X" or a circle on each line to indicate your response. You will not have to compare your answers with anyone else's, and you will not be judged on how well you are doing. This is not a test, but an opportunity for you to chart your own progress in recovery.

| | Not at All | Just a Little | Pretty Much | Very Much |
|---|---|---|---|---|
| 1. I share my needs and wants with others. | | | | |
| 2. I socialize with others. | | | | |
| 3. I stay connected to friends and loved ones. | | | | |
| 4. I nurture my children and/or loved ones. | | | | |
| 5. I am straightforward with others. | | | | |
| 6. I can tell the difference between supportive and non-supportive relationships. | | | | |
| 7. I have developed a support system. | | | | |
| 8. I offer support to others. | | | | |
| 9. I participate in conversations with my family members, friends, and/or coworkers. | | | | |
| 10. I listen to and respect others. | | | | |
| 11. I have clean and sober friends. | | | | |
| 12. I can be trusted. | | | | |

# Reflections on Recovery

In the space below, please write any thoughts, feelings, or questions that you might have about what was covered in this session.

# MODULE C

# Sexuality

This module explores a critical topic in life and recovery. Most of us don't receive a lot of factual education or guidance regarding our sexuality and sexual behavior, yet there are few issues that have a greater impact on our recovery. Sexuality is an essential aspect of the self and an important feature of healthy relationships. Sexuality in recovery is rarely addressed in addiction treatment programs, yet it is one of the most common areas of concern for men and a major cause of relapse. This module looks at the topic from various perspectives, all with the intention of helping people create healthy sexuality that supports their recovery. Having a healthy attitude toward sexuality is possible even for those who are living in a correctional setting.

Sexuality is much more than sexual behavior. It is an identification, a biological drive, an orientation, and an outlook. It includes our perceptions and feelings about ourselves and our perceptions and feelings about others. It involves how we act and with whom we act. Our sexuality reflects our energy, our life forces. So, sexuality is not just about having sex but involves many aspects of the self. Even if you have had healthy and satisfying sexual relationships, you will be able to learn more about your sexual self by participating in this part of the program. If you are not sexually active now, this is still an important area for you to explore.

Just a reminder: When you begin to use this workbook after a group session or on your own, take a minute or two to unwind, relax, and focus on where you are now. Just get settled in the way that feels best for you. Allow yourself to notice how you're breathing and then inhale gently and exhale fully. Repeat the breathing exercise two more times. If you experience difficult feelings during the program, try using one of the grounding activities you are learning in the sessions.

# Sexuality and Addiction

Our sexuality is one of the most basic elements of who we are, but open and honest discussion about sex is frequently discouraged in our society. Most people feel uncomfortable asking questions about sexual matters, so they hear all kinds of confusing and even contradictory messages about sex, about what is okay sexual behavior and what isn't, and about what is okay to discuss and what isn't. For many people, this can create emotions of shame, confusion, embarrassment, and regret, as well as more pleasurable ones.

Being comfortable with our sexuality and coming to terms with our sexual pasts is essential to our physical, emotional, and spiritual well-being. If we feel anxiety, shame, fear, anger, or even confusion about sex, we are at risk of relapse. As we work through the next four sessions, you will begin to discover just how critical sexuality is to a holistic recovery. Healthy sexuality isn't only about having sex. This session can help you to understand your attitudes about sex and how they may be linked to substance use. It also provides a guide for how you might move toward some healthier attitudes about sex.

During the group sessions in this module, your facilitator will have a Question Box available so that you can submit questions about sexual issues. You can write down any question you have, anonymously; fold your paper; and put it in the box.

*A Man's Workbook: Helping Men Recover, A Program for Treating Addiction*, Second Edition.
Stephanie S. Covington, Dan Griffin, and Rick Dauer.
© 2022 Stephanie S. Covington, Dan Griffin, and Rick Dauer. Published 2022 by John Wiley & Sons, Inc.

The goals of this session are

- To begin to feel comfortable discussing sexuality with one another
- To gain basic knowledge and acceptance of one's sexual anatomy, sexual response, and sexual functioning
- To understand that sexual problems are common among some people with substance use disorders

If you are working this program alone, it may help to ask someone to read the instructions for these activities to you the first few times you do them.

# Breathing Activity

This breathing activity includes breathing in for a count of five, holding the breath for a count of five, breathing out for a count of five, and resting for a count of five. It is done four times.

1. Sit in a comfortable position with your feet on the floor.
2. Breathe in and count to five. One, two, three, four, five.
3. Hold it. One, two, three, four, five.
4. Breathe out while counting to five. One, two, three, four, five.
5. Hold again. One, two, three, four, five.
6. Repeat the cycle three more times.

# Focusing on the Here and Now

1. Relax. Take a deep breath.
2. Look at the room around you. Focus on the size of the room.
3. Focus on:
    - the color and texture of the walls
    - the height of the ceilings
    - the lights
    - the windows [if there are any]

- the doors
- the furniture
- the decorations

4. Now focus on yourself.
   - Think of your name.
   - Think of your age.

5. Think of today's date and what time it is.

6. Think of what city and state you are in.

7. Think of the program you are in with this group (if you are in a group).

# A Sexual Health Model

For many addicted people, there is a high correlation between sexual behavior and the use of mood-altering chemicals, and many began exploring sexual activity by themselves and with others at about the same age as they began experimenting with using alcohol or other drugs.

You may have used to overcome shyness or fear of rejection in seeking sexual partners. You may have used in an effort to enhance your sexual performance. You might have engaged in sexual behavior that violated your value system while under the influence. You may have used to deal with feelings of shame or guilt resulting from sexual experiences. You may not have had any sexual experiences without the use of alcohol or other drugs and you may be concerned about what sex will be like when you are in recovery. Finally you may have relapsed, and your relapse may have been due, in part, to sexual issues or behaviors that you never addressed.

Because many people become addicted as teenagers and never have experienced sex while sober, they have not considered the risks, such as unwanted pregnancies; sexually transmitted infections (STIs); and illnesses, including HIV and AIDS. It is important to consider safety in the context of sober sex and to know how to minimize the risks.

Recovery is about being responsible. When we become sober and look back at our behavior, we may be afraid to find out if we have contracted any diseases. It is absolutely critical that you get tested if you have had unprotected sex or engaged in any risky sexual behavior. If you don't know how to go about this, talk to your group facilitator or another counselor and set up a time to meet. Anonymous testing is available, and there are medical therapies that are very effective in curing or managing sexually transmitted illnesses, including HIV and AIDS.

Following is a wheel with ten spokes: ten key characteristics of sexual health.

You will examine many of these components of sexual health in the sessions in this module.

1. *Talking About Sex*. A key part of the Sexual Health Model is the ability to talk comfortably and explicitly about sexuality, especially one's own sexual values, preferences, attractions, history, and behaviors. Being able to talk about sex is necessary and is a valuable skill that must be learned and practiced. There is a simple saying: "If you can't talk about sex, you should not be having it."

2. *Culture and Sexual Identity*. Culture influences one's sexuality and sense of sexual self. It is important to examine your culture as it influences your sexual identity, attitudes, behaviors, and health.

# Sexual Health Model

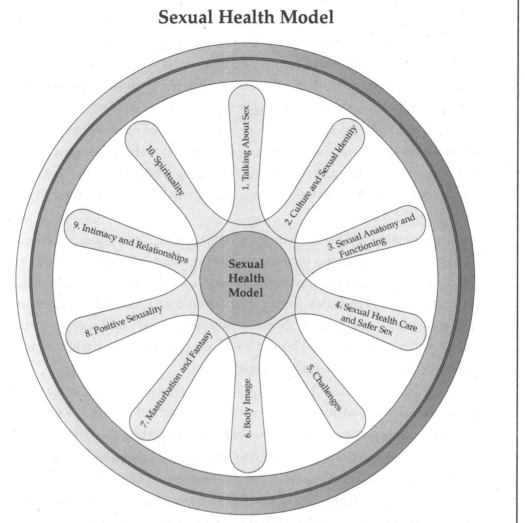

Source: "The Sexual Health Model: Application of a Sexological Approach to HIV Prevention," by B. Robinson, W. O. Bockting, S. Rosser, D. L. Rugg, M. Miner, and E. Coleman, 2002. *Health Education Research: Theory and Practice, 17(1)*, pp. 43–57. Copyright 2002 by Oxford University Press. Adapted with permission.

3. *Sexual Anatomy and Functioning.* Sexual health assumes a basic understanding and acceptance of one's sexual anatomy, sexual response, and sexual functioning. Sexual health includes freedom from sexual dysfunction and other sexual problems.

4. *Sexual Health Care and Safer Sex.* Sexual health involves knowing one's body, performing regular self-exams for cancer and STDs, and responding to physical changes with appropriate medical intervention. Take care of your body, and your body will take care of you.

5. *Challenges: Overcoming Barriers to Sexual Health.* Challenges to sexual health are sexual abuse, addiction, compulsive sexual behavior, sex work, harassment, and

discrimination. Because many men are pushed toward unhealthy sexual attitudes and behaviors, we have to confront them directly as we explore sexual health.

6. *Body Image.* In a culture obsessed with a type of physical beauty that few of us will ever achieve, a realistic, positive body image is an important aspect of sexual health. This can be difficult to achieve. Challenging the notion of one, narrow standard of beauty and encouraging self-acceptance is relevant to all populations.

7. *Masturbation and Fantasy.* In our culture, the topics of masturbation and fantasy are surrounded by misunderstanding and confusion, because most of us do not grow up exposed to healthy conversations about these subjects. However, they can be part of healthy sexuality when they are in balance with the rest of the spokes in the model.

8. *Positive Sexuality.* All human beings need to explore their sexuality in order to develop and nurture who they are. Exploring and celebrating sexuality from a positive and self-affirming perspective is an essential feature of sexual health. Positive sexuality includes appropriate experimentation; affirming sensuality; attaining sexual competence through the ability to give and receive sexual pleasure; and setting sexual boundaries based on what one prefers as well as what one knows is safe and responsible.

9. *Intimacy and Relationships.* Intimacy is a universal need that people try to meet through their relationships. There are different kinds of intimacy. Knowing which intimacy needs are important for you is helpful in getting these needs met.

10. *Spirituality.* Our definition of sexual health assumes that a person's ethical, spiritual, and moral beliefs and his sexual behaviors and values are aligned. In this context, spirituality may not include religion, but it needs to address moral and ethical concerns and deeper values. This helps us to integrate our sexual and spiritual selves.

At first, it can be extremely difficult to talk about sex in an open and honest manner within your group. You may not be sure what to say and what not to say. You may have some very painful or confusing memories and feelings about your sexuality. In our society, open and honest discussion about sex is frequently discouraged. You may be relieved that others have had some of the same experiences you have had. Maybe you are glad that you have finally found a place where you can be open about your questions. Whatever you're feeling is absolutely valid and important.

If you are using this workbook individually, it will be of benefit to talk to your counselor or other advisor (if you have access to one) about any questions or other issues that come up for you during the sessions in this module.

# Discussion Questions

1. How did you first learn about sex?

2. Who in your life can you talk to about sex in an open and honest manner?

3. How does it feel to talk about sex with others in the group setting?

4. What are your concerns about being sexual as a person in recovery?

# The Sexual-Chemical Lifeline

The Sexual-Chemical Lifeline is a way to begin seeing the relationship between your use of alcohol or other drugs and your sexual behaviors. As you look back at your past to identify your sexual experiences, you may remember events that you had previously forgotten or you may be surprised at how painful some of your memories are. You may become aware of certain patterns, especially patterns between chemical and sexual activities. It is not uncommon to find that, as your addiction progressed, your sexual experiences became less pleasant. You also may find that certain sexual behaviors were associated with a lot of alcohol and/or drug use.

By charting your Sexual-Chemical Lifeline, you can begin to become more aware of your sexual self when you were drinking or using. Then you can start thinking about your sexual self in recovery and consider what changes you would like to make.

You do not need to rush through this. The group members' lifelines are reviewed in Session 17.

The following is a sample Sexual-Chemical Lifeline for a person named Tom.

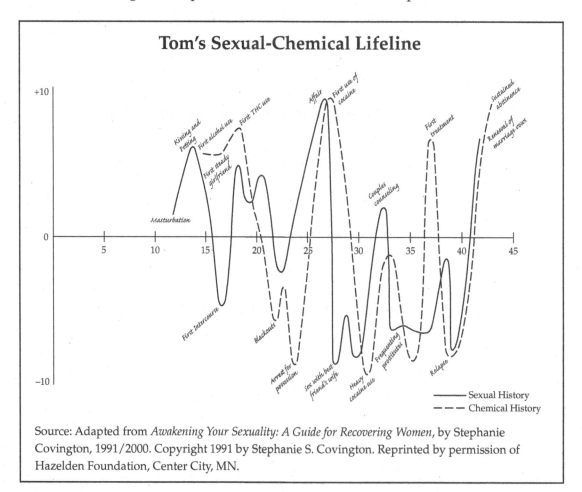

Source: Adapted from *Awakening Your Sexuality: A Guide for Recovering Women*, by Stephanie Covington, 1991/2000. Copyright 1991 by Stephanie S. Covington. Reprinted by permission of Hazelden Foundation, Center City, MN.

On the sample lifeline, you can see that the straight horizontal line is the baseline. It is marked 5, 10, 15, and so on. Those numbers represent the person's age.

On the left side of the chart is a vertical line labeled +10, 0, and −10. Events that are pleasant experiences fall in the 0 to +10 range, from okay to really great. Painful events fall in the 0 to −10 range. The more painful the event, the closer it is to −10.

Looking at the sample lifeline, you can see that Tom's highest sexual point was an affair, and it coincided with his most pleasurable drug experience, when he was introduced to cocaine. Notice that both lines drop dramatically from there to very low points, as his addiction went out of control and was linked to an experience of increased infidelity, including an affair with his best friend's wife.

1. Use the chart on the next page to create your own Sexual-Chemical Lifeline. Start by charting your history of addiction. Before the next session, draw your history of using alcohol and/or other drugs as a broken line.
2. After that, draw your sexual history as a solid line. Then look to see how your history of addiction and your sexual history have affected each other.

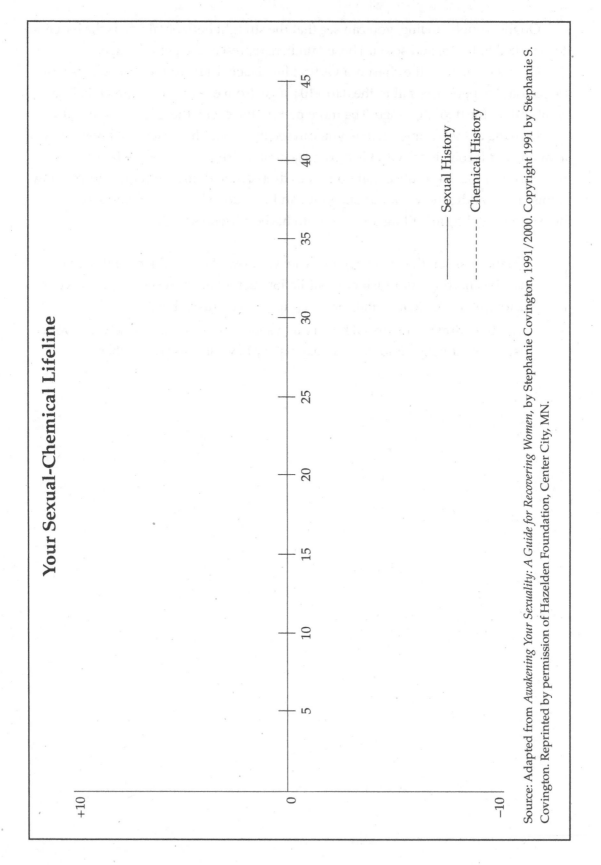

## Your Sexual-Chemical Lifeline

+10

0

−10

5    10    15    20    25    30    35    40    45

—————— Sexual History

-------- Chemical History

Source: Adapted from *Awakening Your Sexuality: A Guide for Recovering Women*, by Stephanie Covington, 1991/2000. Copyright 1991 by Stephanie S. Covington. Reprinted by permission of Hazelden Foundation, Center City, MN.

*Helping Men Recover A Man's Workbook*

# Between-Sessions Activities

1. Your assignment for next session is to continue working on your Sexual-Chemical Lifeline.

2. In addition, please complete the initial Recovery Scale for this module.

## Recovery Scale: Sexuality

Please take a few moments to mark the degree to which you do each of the following things. Make an "X" or a circle on each line to indicate your response. You will not have to compare your answers with anyone else's, and you will not be judged on how well you are doing. This is not a test, but an opportunity for you to chart your own progress in recovery.

| | Not at All | Just a Little | Pretty Much | Very Much |
|---|---|---|---|---|
| 1. I am comfortable with my body. | | | | |
| 2. I can talk to professionals, including my counselor and my doctor, about sexual concerns. | | | | |
| 3. I can speak appropriately with other people about sexual matters. | | | | |
| 4. I can be affectionate with others. | | | | |
| 5. I am comfortable with my sexual identity. | | | | |
| 6. I am comfortable with my gender identity. | | | | |
| 7. I can accept sexual pleasure from my partner. | | | | |
| 8. I consider my partner's sexual needs and preferences. | | | | |
| 9. I can express my sexual desires to my partner. | | | | |
| 10. I am comfortable having sober sex. | | | | |
| 11. I believe that pleasing myself sexually is healthy. | | | | |
| 12. I understand that sexuality is about more than the physical act of sex. | | | | |

# Reflections on Recovery

In the space below, please write any thoughts, feelings, or questions that you might have about what was covered in this session.

# Sexual Identity

Many people begin using alcohol or other drugs in adolescence or earlier, usually at the time that they are exploring their sexuality. Experimenting sexually with a variety of people and situations can be a natural part of healthy development. However, the use of alcohol and other drugs can interfere with the development of sexuality in many areas, including confusion regarding sexual orientation and gender identity. Some people have sexual encounters with others of the same sex while they are under the influence and then wonder what that means about their sexuality and about their relationships with other men.

Also, many unhealthy aspects of male sexuality are rooted in the socialization process and The Man Rules. In this session, you explore some of the social messages sent to both men and women by families, communities, cultures, religions, one's peers, and the media. A lot of these messages are negative or reinforce unhealthy sexuality. People who grow up in a modern society often emerge from the socialization process with confusing messages about sex, lack of education about sexual and gender issues, and negative perceptions of their bodies.

The sessions in this module will help you to examine various aspects of sexuality, including the messages you may have assimilated about sexuality.

*A Man's Workbook: Helping Men Recover, A Program for Treating Addiction,* Second Edition.
Stephanie S. Covington, Dan Griffin, and Rick Dauer.
© 2022 Stephanie S. Covington, Dan Griffin, and Rick Dauer. Published 2022 by John Wiley & Sons, Inc.

The goals of this session are

- To understand the continuum of masculine and feminine characteristics
- To understand the continuum of sexual identity
- To look at our judgments of and beliefs about people who identify as LGBTQI+
- To understand how heterosexism, sexual prejudice, transphobia, and similar biases affect our self-perceptions, our perceptions of masculinity, and our relationships

# The Question Box

If anything from the Question Box is of interest to you, you may want to make some notes here.

# Social Messages About Sexuality and Gender

Please consider your experiences and attitudes growing up regarding individuals who are lesbian, gay, bisexual, transgender, gender nonbinary, or those who are questioning or identify as queer – also known as LGBTQI+. This discussion is not about convincing anyone to believe one thing or another. When it comes to the topic of LGBTQI+ issues, there remains a lot of stigma and misunderstanding even as social, scientific, and behavioral understanding and messages continue to evolve. The goal here is for all participants to have a chance to reflect on what they have believed directly or indirectly about this topic and to see how it has affected them and their relationships. Just as with every other session, we encourage respect for each person in the group and everything that is contributed to the discussion and activities. This is an opportunity for all participants to stretch their comfort zones and to be open with their attitudes, outlooks, and experiences while also showing compassion and respect.

## Discussion Questions

1. What did you hear or believe about LGBTQI+ individuals when you were a child? When you were an adolescent?

2. What have you heard or believed about LGBTQI+ people as an adult?

3. If you do not identify as LGBTQI+, imagine that you do. What do you think would be a challenge for you in your life?

4. If you do identify as LGBTQI+, what would you like us to know?

# Masculine and Feminine Traits

Unfortunately, most people raised as boys learn very early that they shouldn't be "feminine" or "sissy." They are taught to ignore, dislike, and hide the feminine parts of themselves. This is reinforced by being teased, mocked, humiliated, and even physically harmed when they don't. Yet every person has some degree of nurturing or artistic or other so-called "feminine" characteristics. If you get emotional while watching sad movies, you are no less a man than one who does not like such movies. There is nothing wrong with liking poetry, being artistic, knowing how to cook, or watching competitive dance shows! Unfortunately, trying to avoid all so-called feminine aspects of ourselves results in our disliking, or even being ashamed of, certain valuable parts of ourselves. This is one of the primary reasons that many men struggle with fully accepting every aspect of who they are, and it is one of the primary reasons that many men have so much trouble developing intimate relationships with other men.

It also leads us to devalue women. We diminish their value and their abilities because we do not value those parts of ourselves. Most of the time, we are not even aware that we are doing this. It is this process that also contributes to the devaluing of any intimate-partner relationship that is not a traditional opposite-sex relationship. This overlooks the fact that love is love and that all safe, healthy relationships between consenting adults have value.

We tend to think of masculinity and femininity as rigid categories; however, research shows that they exist on a continuum. All people have a combination of both masculine and feminine traits. We can be on different parts of the continuum at different times in different relationships. There is more freedom now in how individuals express themselves. Some people express a different type of masculinity when they are with family members than they do when they are with co-workers or playing sports. Many of the greatest chefs have been men; many of the greatest artists and poets and composers have been men. Today, it is not at all uncommon for a man to wear a pink or purple shirt. And there are a lot more men who take care of children and do housework.

1. What are some of the qualities, traits, affinities (meaning things we like naturally), and behaviors that we identify as being masculine in nature?

2. How have The Man Rules limited your concept of masculinity?

3. What are some of the qualities, traits, affinities, and behaviors that we identify as being feminine in nature?

4. What traits, skills, or interests that often are labeled "feminine" do you think can contribute to a man being more well-rounded?

# Heterosexism, Sexual Prejudice, and Misogyny

Now let's consider sexual orientation. Heterosexuals identify as being attracted to people of the other sex than their own: male or female. Gay men and lesbians identify as being attracted to people who are of the same sex as their own. Bisexuals are attracted to people of either sex. These orientations also exist on a continuum.

In the 1940s, Alfred Kinsey and his colleagues interviewed about ten thousand people and found that very few people are entirely heterosexual or entirely gay or homosexual. Only a few of the participants in the study were zeros or sixes on a scale of zero to six. The vast majority were somewhere between one and five. Subsequent studies by other sexuality researchers have substantiated these results. It also has been demonstrated that an individual's sexual orientation can change over time. In addition, some people who are definitively heterosexual may have same-sex experiences under certain conditions, such as being incarcerated.

Since early childhood, you probably have been exposed to a wide variety of opinions about gay men, and many of them were probably negative. If you are gay, these messages may have caused you to hide your sexual preferences from others or to feel ashamed of who you are. If you are heterosexual, these messages may have caused you to feel compelled to prove to others (and perhaps to yourself) that you are straight.

There are gay men who are very masculine. There are heterosexual men who exhibit and embrace various feminine characteristics. But because of the way in which we generally treat boys and young men who exhibit any feminine characteristics, we ensure that some young men keep those qualities hidden. This results in young people growing up hiding core parts of themselves from themselves and others. Imagine how this can impact a trans person.

Some of you might be afraid of or feel anger and contempt toward others whom you think are gay or transgender. Anger or scorn toward those who are gay, lesbian, or bisexual is called "sexual prejudice." It is an attitude based on hostility, fear, and dislike and is directed at whole groups of people. Discrimination or prejudice against gay people on the assumption that heterosexuality is the normal or better sexual orientation is called "heterosexism." Sexual prejudice and heterosexism are at the core of much of the discrimination, adversity, abuse, and violence that people of the LGBTQI+ community have endured. Transphobia describes the experience that many transgender and nonbinary people have.

Some individuals' attitudes or beliefs about sexuality are rooted in religious doctrine. This program does not wish to challenge anyone's religious beliefs. What simply ask that you be honest about your own thoughts and feelings and that you be respectful of others' thoughts and feelings.

On a deeper individual level, sexual prejudice stems from a fear of one's own ambivalent sexuality. For many men, it may manifest as fear of having any affection for or friendships with other men. Because many men confuse intimacy with sexuality, sexual prejudice is a primary factor in the difficulty that heterosexual men have in developing close relationships with one another.

You may be gay or transgender and afraid to acknowledge it because of the social stigma, threats of being ostracized, or fear of violence. You may be afraid that you are gay because you are sensitive and emotional. You may have friends or children who are lesbian, gay, bisexual, transgender, or nonbinary and not know how to be open about it with them. You may be gay, bisexual, transgender, or nonbinary and comfortable with that part of your identity—whether you have shared that with this group or not. Remember that feelings of shame about who we are put us at high risk of returning to the use of alcohol or other drugs.

Finally, look at the list you created earlier of feminine characteristics. Some men treat people who have feminine characteristics with negativity and abuse. That is called sexism or misogyny. Literally, it means the hatred of women or that which we associate with women. Of course, it shows up in varying degrees. Consider the problems that women have in getting certain jobs, getting pay that is equal to men's, dealing with people such as mechanics and builders, and so on. It is very sad that anyone rejects the feminine aspect, which is a core part of all of us.

1. How safe and comfortable do you feel talking about sexual orientation, and sexual identity, and gender identity?

2. What feelings have you had as the result of this session?

3. Did this session explore any issues that you would like to discuss with your counselor, advisor, or another professional?

This may have been a difficult session for you. You probably have not had much previous opportunity to explore some of these issues. You may have been raised to have strong feelings about sexuality and sexual practices. You may even have been told that it isn't proper to have these kinds of discussions.

Beliefs about sexuality can be influenced by age, religious tradition, cultural background, and socioeconomic class. The goal of this session is simply to provide you with an opportunity to consider new information and ideas, to help you establish your own comfort zone with your sexuality, and to better understand the differences in sexuality that others experience.

# Body Image

How we accept, respect, and take care of our bodies indicates and affects how we feel about our sexuality. Feeling adequate and accepting of their bodies is difficult for most people, although we rarely talk about it. Unfortunately, our society places a great deal of importance on how people look.

As children, some of us were smaller than others, some were overweight, and some were teased about other physical things. The effects that negative ideas about our bodies have on us extend into adulthood. If a child's body is connected to verbal or physical abuse at home and/or in school, this only makes it worse.

Because we have grown up in a culture dominated by television, magazines, films, and social media, we often compare our bodies to those who have been judged as perfect or sexy. Even their bodies usually aren't good enough naturally; they may need hours of time in the gym every day at the expense of other important parts of life. Some are altered with drugs and surgery. Many are photographed with makeup and with special camera lenses. Then the photographs are touched up by computer programs before we see them.

Most people, even those considered attractive or in shape, feel bad about some parts of their bodies. For men, it may be their weight, height, hair color or type (or loss of hair), their muscles, or their penis size. They begin to dislike and feel ashamed of their bodies rather than appreciating what their bodies do for them. Those who are judged to be good looking and the "ideal" type may have to work to maintain their bodies and may feel a lot of pressure if they believe that without the good looks and the toned bodies, they aren't desirable. For some, including trans individuals, no matter what they do, it doesn't work because they are not in the "right" bodies. Those individuals have a special issue with their bodies.

In regard to penis size, it is amazing that something that is such a small part of the body has such influence over how a man feels about himself. The average erect penis is five and one-half to six and one-half inches long, irrespective of its size when flaccid or the man's ethnicity. Some are smaller, and some are bigger. Many men have some insecurity about their penis size or shape or its ability to satisfy their partners, although in study after study, the vast majority of people said that they were very satisfied with their partners' sizes or that it simply didn't matter. For those who engage in sex with women, it may be good to know that, although a woman's vagina may stretch to accommodate any size penis, it is only naturally four inches deep when a woman is sexually aroused.

A man's sense of masculinity is deeply connected to his penis, his ability to maintain erections, and knowing that he can use his penis to please others. According

154         

to The Man Rules, if the body is a machine, one's penis is the main component that determines the value of the machine. As a result, sex is a task that the machine performs. If the penis works, the machine is good; if the penis does not work, the machine is broken and not valuable.

The reality is that we all have different bodies, and our bodies change over time. We gain weight and lose weight; our hair changes color and falls out; our ability to achieve erection may be compromised. We are continually challenged to come to terms with aging, disease, and other factors that affect our bodies.

The most important thing is how you accept your body, not the judgment of others. Many people who use alcohol or other drugs neglect their bodies or are trying to avoid dealing with body-image issues. It is important for people in recovery to learn to love, respect, and accept their bodies, whatever their sizes, shapes, ages, or types. This is a process that takes time. You cannot just will this to happen. Of course, there may be aspects of your body, such as excess weight, that you can change if you are motivated to do so.

# Between-Sessions Activities

1. Your first assignment to do between now and the next session may sound odd or make you uncomfortable at first, but it may help you to try it. Stand naked in front of a mirror and look at your body. Notice what thoughts and judgments come up. Notice the parts of your body that you like. Notice the parts of your body that you do not like.

2. On the following page are two outlines of a person's body. The first represents the front of your body, and the second represents the back of your body. Use these drawings to indicate your feelings about the different parts of your body. Fill in these figures by marking them in one of three ways:

   • Mark the parts of your body that you like and feel satisfied with by using plus signs, like this:

     + + + + +

   • Mark the parts you do not like, hate, or feel uncomfortable with by using minus signs, like this:

     – – – – –

   • Mark the parts of your body that you feel neutral about by using little circles, like this:

     o o o o o

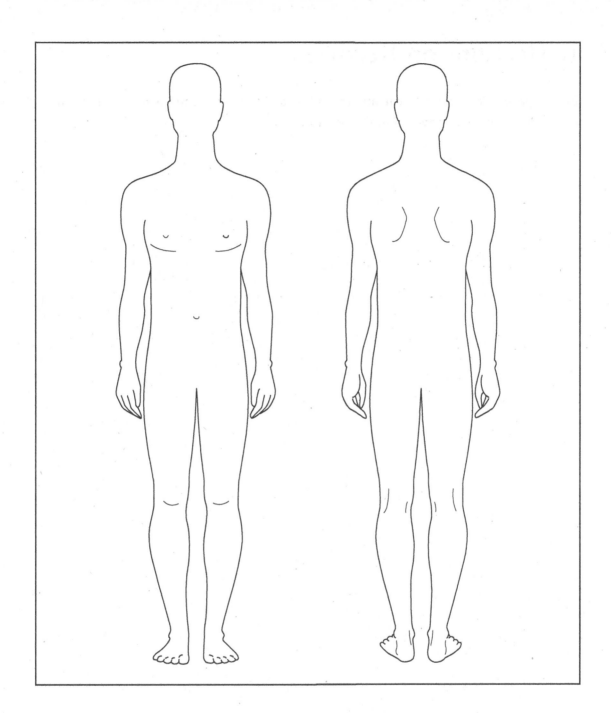

3. Also, please continue working on your Sexual-Chemical Lifeline.

# Reflections on Recovery

In the space below, please write any thoughts, feelings, or questions that you might have about what was covered in this session.

# Barriers to Sexual Health

This session explores the many barriers people encounter in their efforts to establish healthy sexuality. The previous session asserted that our ideas about sexuality are shaped by the way we are socialized by our culture. This session looks at the harmful effects of that socialization by identifying various problematic sexual behaviors. For example, many men have been raised to view sex, and women, in a distorted way. For men, sex can be combined with many things, such as power, love, control, intimacy, and masculinity. When sex is combined with power, control, insecurity, and shame, it can become a tool to hurt others. One of the most deeply meaningful ways of connecting with another human being and expressing our love also has the potential to cause a great deal of pain. Add alcohol and other drugs to the mix, and the potential for harm increases. Many people also mistakenly believe that the use of alcohol and other drugs enhances sexual desire and performance.

This session also provides an opportunity for your group to talk as openly as possible about your fears of being sexually active while sober and to begin to identify some of your relapse triggers.

The goals of this session are

- To understand some of the significant barriers to having healthy sexual relationships
- To look at potential relapse triggers related to sexuality
- To recognize the full spectrum of nonconsensual sexual behavior
- To explore what constitutes consensual versus nonconsensual sex

*A Man's Workbook: Helping Men Recover, A Program for Treating Addiction,* Second Edition.
Stephanie S. Covington, Dan Griffin, and Rick Dauer.
© 2022 Stephanie S. Covington, Dan Griffin, and Rick Dauer. Published 2022 by John Wiley & Sons, Inc.

# The Question Box

If anything from the Question Box is of interest to you, you may want to make some notes here.

# Sex While Under the Influence

For many addicted people, there is a high correlation between sexual behavior and the use of mood-altering chemicals. You may have used alcohol or other drugs to overcome shyness or fear of rejection in seeking sexual partners. You may have used in an effort to enhance your sexual performance. You may have engaged in sexual behavior that violated your value system while under the influence. You may have used alcohol or other drugs to deal with feelings of shame or guilt resulting from sexual experiences. You may not have had any sexual experiences without the use of alcohol or drugs, and you may be concerned about what sex will be like when you are in recovery.

One of the most common myths that people believe is that using alcohol and other drugs will improve their sex lives. You may have felt more attractive and more confident while under the influence. You may have felt that being high improved your sexual performance. In fact, most mood-altering chemicals have long-term, negative effects on sexuality and sexual performance.

*Alcohol:* Alcohol use generally lowers inhibitions, and people are more likely to initiate or be receptive to sexual activity while intoxicated. Yet the more alcohol an individual consumes, the more likely he is to experience sexual problems, such as erectile dysfunction and either premature or delayed ejaculation. Alcohol is a depressant of the central nervous system, and healthy sexual functioning is related to a healthy nervous system. Long-term alcohol use is associated with lowered testosterone levels and decreased sexual desire. Alcohol use impairs an individual's ability to make healthy decisions about sexual activity. Alcohol has also been shown to increase aggression in some individuals, which can lead to violence and forcing others to engage in nonconsensual sexual activities.

*Marijuana:* Marijuana appears to have little direct effect on sexual functioning. However, chronic use has been linked to decreased sperm production. People sometimes believe that marijuana will improve sex, but, in general, both men and women report decreased sexual desire when using marijuana.

*Cocaine:* Many men believe that cocaine sexually excites women and that it improves the ability to maintain erections. Low doses of cocaine seem to increase testosterone levels, but higher doses have the opposite effect. Cocaine activates the pleasure centers in the brain in ways that are similar to the ways in which sex affects the brain. Thus, using cocaine can trigger a desire for sex, and engaging in sexual activity can stimulate a desire to use the drug. Chronic use of cocaine may lead to decreased sexual desire, erectile dysfunction, and delayed orgasm.

*Methamphetamine:* Methamphetamines do not seem to have a direct effect on sexual functioning in low doses. Higher doses and chronic use may lead to decreased libido and erectile dysfunction. The drug initially enhances a person's sense of general well-being and excitement, which may lower sexual inhibitions. Methamphetamine use is linked to high-risk sexual behaviors, including violence. Intravenous use increases the risk of exposure to HIV. Long-term use is physically debilitating and results in decreased sexual desire and functioning.

*Heroin:* Heroin and other opiate drugs (such as morphine, methadone, codeine, OxyContin, and oxycodone) lower the metabolic rate and tend to suppress sexual desire and functioning. Intravenous use increases the risk of exposure to HIV and hepatitis. Chronic opiate users consistently report an inability to maintain an erection and achieve orgasm.

Although alcohol and other drugs can increase sexual response initially, chronic use tends to deteriorate all areas of sexual response for both men and women. For an addict, the physical, emotional, and behavioral damage of chemical use inevitably has a negative effect on sexuality and sexual functioning.

# Harmful Sexual Behaviors

Alcohol and other drug use can have serious effects on sexual behavior. Following are some common problematic and harmful behaviors that may result from addiction to alcohol and other drugs.

- Sexual harassment
- Taking advantage of an inebriated or drugged partner
- Date rape
- Sexual abuse
- Infidelity, having affairs
- Unprotected sex
- Other risky sexual behaviors
- Using drugs to enhance sexual experiences
- Compulsive sexual behavior
- Avoiding intimacy other than physical interaction
- Neglecting a partner's needs and desires
- Avoiding physical relationships
- Dishonest or manipulative actions to have sex
- Using sex to dominate or otherwise control others
- Going along with a peer group's behavior in violation of one's personal values
- Using alcohol and other drugs to give oneself permission to act out sexually

# Sex and Consent

One definition of healthy sexual relationships is "Anything is okay as long as it's between two or more consenting adults and does not create harm." Let's think about the word "consenting." We know that rape is never consensual, but there are other sexual acts that you may not have thought of as being nonconsensual. Here are some examples of nonconsensual sex:

- Putting drugs in someone's drink in order to make the person compliant
- Using authority or power to coerce someone into having sex
- Not stopping when a person says "No"
- Threatening to withhold economic support unless sexual demands are met
- Employing verbal or emotional abuse to manipulate someone into having sex
- Employing physical threats or violence
- Threatening to terminate the relationship unless sexual demands are met

It's important to understand that if there is a significant age difference or power difference in a relationship, it is really difficult for the relationship to be healthy or consensual. Sex with children under the age of consent is always abuse.

When using, you may have engaged in sexual behavior that you now feel sorry about. You may have confused desire with intimacy or love. Acknowledging these memories will help begin the process of healing. You may want to talk privately with a counselor or another professional person about some of these behaviors.

# Masturbation

A sexual behavior that can be quite confusing for people is masturbation. It is rarely discussed and almost universally practiced. From the onset of puberty throughout adulthood and into old age, people masturbate. Even those who are in sexually fulfilling relationships masturbate. People do it for a variety of reasons: to relieve stress, to help themselves fall asleep, to experience pleasure, and to explore their own sexuality. Masturbation for any of these reasons is not harmful or unhealthy.

An advantage of masturbation for many individuals is that it is a convenient way of experiencing sexual pleasure without having to dedicate much time or effort—no partner necessary, no need for consent from another, no conversation, no need to be concerned about another person's pleasure, and no emotional investment.

Although this may sound somewhat selfish, there is nothing wrong with deriving private pleasure from one's own body. Masturbation is frequently accompanied by sexual fantasy, which means imagining other sexual acts, some of which may be completely out of the realm of possibility. There is nothing deviant or harmful about this, so long as the fantasies do not involve children or coercion of others. Having sexual fantasies is an important component of healthy sexuality. Some people feel guilt, shame, and confusion about masturbation when, in fact, their behavior is normal.

However, anything can become unhealthy if it's out of balance. It is psychologically unhealthy for a person to masturbate compulsively as a remedy for loneliness, to avoid the risk of interpersonal sexual relationships, and/or to cope with other unpleasant emotional states.

There are some religious taboos against masturbation. While we assert that it can be a normal and healthy practice, we also understand that some people will have been taught that masturbation is sinful. It is up to you to determine what is right for you in this area and in all areas of sexual practice.

# Sexual Triggers and Relapse

The first months or years of recovery can be quite challenging. A lot of negative feelings may come up. Many of these feelings would have led you to using in the past. Now you have made the decision to no longer use alcohol or other drugs as a coping mechanism. It is not unusual to turn to some form of sex to help you deal with your feelings. The problem is that you may be in danger of substituting one set of addictive or harmful behaviors for another. And even engaging in healthy sexual activity may be a relapse trigger (or "activator") for you.

Addiction causes chemical changes in the brain. Your brain became accustomed to the pleasurable feelings generated by alcohol or other drugs. Now that the chemicals are gone, your brain still wants to feel a certain way. Sex can help to provide those pleasurable feelings or take uncomfortable feelings away, because the chemical release that accompanies sex might remind your brain of using. So sexual activity in early recovery could trigger the desire to use again. Another risk is that you may not find sexual activities as intense as they were when you were using, so you might feel a desire to get drunk or high in order to recapture that physical sensation. Finally, you may not have much experience initiating or consummating sexual activity when you are sober. The fear of rejection, loneliness, or inadequate performance might make you crave a chemical boost.

# Discussion Questions

Whether you are using this workbook in a group or individually, think about the implications of these three questions for you. You may want to make some notes here. You also may want to discuss them with your counselor or other advisor (if you have access to one).

1. "What attitudes or sexual behaviors from your past might pose a threat to your recovery?"

   Here are two examples of triggers from the past: "I used to go to topless clubs with my friends. If I were to do that now, it would definitely cause cravings to drink." Or "I used to think it was okay to lie to someone in order to get them into bed. If I were to do that now, it would make me feel guilty and ashamed of myself."

2. "What attitudes or sexual behaviors occurring currently could pose a threat to your recovery?"

   Here is an example of this kind of trigger: "Right now I am not comfortable dating and I am avoiding all possible sexual opportunities. If this continues for much longer, I am going to get really lonely and frustrated." Here's another: "I don't know where to meet potential sexual partners. If I don't figure this out, I will be tempted to start going back to bars and other drinking or using environments."

3. "What attitudes or sexual behaviors might occur in the future that could potentially pose a threat to your recovery?"

For example: "I used drugs practically every time I had sex and I relied on them to aid my performance. If I find that I can't perform or enjoy sex as much without drugs, I will be tempted to use them again." Another example is this: "I like having a variety of sexual partners. In the past, I could do that and not feel guilty. But now I realize that I want something more in my relationships than just sex. I want to be in a committed relationship. But what if I get sexually bored? How will I deal with that?"

# Sober Sex

Most people in early recovery are concerned about what it will be like to be sexual without the aid of alcohol or other drugs. Will it be any good? Will I be able to last as long as I did when I was high? Where will I meet sober sexual partners? Will anyone find me sexually attractive? If you have been having such concerns, you are not alone. Any feelings of insecurity that you may have about sex become more apparent to you when you are sober and chemicals are not masking your fears. You may begin to think you are doomed to having no sex, not enough sex, or unsatisfying sex for the rest of your life. Talking about these fears and concerns with other recovering people will go a long way toward helping you feel more comfortable and confident. It also will help you begin to create a new, healthy, and satisfying sexual life for yourself.

# Sexual Addiction/Compulsivity

Some people who have problems with alcohol or other drugs have a concurrent sexual addiction or compulsivity. Others might develop a sexual addiction after becoming sober. Sexual compulsivity is characterized by repetitive and intense sexual fantasies, sexual urges, and/or sexual behaviors that cause negative consequences in one's social life, job, and other important areas of life. Examples of behaviors that could lead to or indicate sexual addiction/compulsion are masturbating excessively; using pornography excessively; compulsively looking for a sexual partner; being fixated on a sexual partner; having excessive sex within a relationship; constantly seeking more intense sexual experiences; using sex services (such as telephone lines, strip clubs, massage parlors, and prostitutes) excessively; and frequently moving from one sexual relationship to another.

There are therapists, programs, and mutual support groups available for people who struggle with sexual addiction/compulsion. If you have concerns about this topic, please see your facilitator or another counselor, so that you can be helped to find some appropriate resources.

# Between-Sessions Activities

1. This is your last opportunity to work on your Sexual Chemical Lifeline. By now, you should have it done or almost done. You will have an opportunity to share your lifelines in the next session.

   This has been another full session. You have considered some pretty heavy aspects of sex. You may be feeling some discomfort, and that is perfectly natural. You also may be feeling some relief in realizing that you are not the only one who has confusion or fear about this topic. You may feel less alone because some of the things you have felt ashamed of were discussed by the others.

2. This week, make it a point to do some things that are fun. Stay in close contact with your friends, sponsors, and/or counselors. Go to extra meetings if you can. Also take some time to be with yourself. There can be a delay in experiencing the impact of these heavy conversations. It can catch you off guard. So just be aware of how you are feeling between now and our next session and reach out for help when you need to.

# Reflections on Recovery

In the space below, please write any thoughts, feelings, or questions that you might have about what was covered in this session.

# Healthy Sexuality

You and your group members have worked through some difficult, and perhaps painful, discussions related to sex and your ideas about sex. It is not easy for most people who identify as men to talk about healthy sexuality and love. Romantic love requires many to let go of some of the key concepts of "masculinity," and this scares them. For many, sex has taken the place of love and intimacy. This session can help you to consider how the issues of love, intimacy, and sex are different and also related.

This session offers you a new way of looking at sex and sexuality. It offers you an opportunity to define what healthy sexuality might look like for you. You have more ability to choose how sexuality fits into your life than you may have imagined. Developing healthy sexuality can improve your relationships and your life, and you deserve this.

The goals of this session are

- To explore aspects of sexual development
- To understand that love and sex can be two connected but separate concepts
- To begin to create a concept of healthy sexuality

*A Man's Workbook: Helping Men Recover, A Program for Treating Addiction,* Second Edition.
Stephanie S. Covington, Dan Griffin, and Rick Dauer.
© 2022 Stephanie S. Covington, Dan Griffin, and Rick Dauer. Published 2022 by John Wiley & Sons, Inc.

# The Question Box

If anything from the Question Box is of interest to you, you may want to make some notes here.

# Sharing Sexual-Chemical Lifelines

1. What has this activity has been like for you? What realizations have you had?

2. What have you learned about the relationship between sexuality and addiction?

# Collage of Healthy Sexuality

A collage is usually paper and other materials glued onto a backing. Like other art, the technique of collage uses visual imagery to express what is not always easy to express in words. As an opportunity to express healthy sexuality in a creative way, you can create a collage to represent your vision of your ideal sexual self.

To make your collage, you need a piece of poster board or large cardboard, at least two magazines (not news magazines), a pair of scissors, and a glue stick.

You cut or tear out pictures and words that represent your vision of sexual health and glue them to the poster board or cardboard. If you see a picture in a magazine that "speaks" to you, use it. Try not to think too hard about it. Remember that recovery is about growth and expansion—about letting go of some of the old rules about what we can do and not do. Take the risk of allowing yourself to play, have fun, be creative, and see what happens.

When you have finished your collage, here are some things to think about:

1. Why did you choose the words and images that you did?

2. How does this represent your vision of healthy sexuality?

# A Sexual Health Model

You may remember from pages 136 through 138 that the Sexual Health Model is a wheel with ten spokes—the ten key characteristics of sexual health.

1. *Talking About Sex.* What does that mean to you?

2. *Culture and Sexual Identity.* What does that mean to you?

3. *Sexual Anatomy and Functioning.* What does that mean to you?

4. *Sexual Health Care and Safer Sex.* What does that mean to you?

5. *Overcoming Barriers to Sexual Health.* What does that mean to you?

6. *Body Image.* What does that mean to you?

7. *Masturbation and Fantasy.* What does that mean to you?

8. *Positive Sexuality.* What does that mean to you?

9. *Intimacy and Relationships.* What does that mean to you?

10. *Spirituality*. What does that mean to you?




Is there anything missing from this list that you can think of?




Is there anything that you think does not belong?

# Love, Sex, and Intimacy

Love is perhaps the most gratifying and most complicated of human emotions. We look for and need love more than we may be willing to admit. People often think of love as a feeling, but love is also a behavior. Feeling love is easy, but being a loving person is much more difficult. Three things are necessary for love: respect, mutuality, and compassion.

1. *Respect* is the appreciation of another's abilities, values, qualities, and achievements. Respect is characterized by attentiveness, consideration, and thoughtfulness, and it is essential in a love relationship. We earn respect when we act according to our values and principles.

2. *Mutuality* means that there is an equal investment in the relationship. Each person has a willingness and desire to "see" the other as well as to be seen; to hear the other as well as to be heard; and to be vulnerable as well as to respect the other's vulnerability. Mutuality also means that there is an awareness of the "we," not merely of the two individuals.

3. *Compassion* is similar to empathy but it occurs on a deeper level. Empathy is understanding another's feeling and being able to feel along with the person. Compassion is caring deeply about another person's struggle or pain and wanting to help alleviate it. When we are compassionate, we lend ourselves to another's process; we give of ourselves in order to be with the other person emotionally.

When these three qualities are present, sex is different from what many of us are raised to experience or want. Sometimes what you really want from your partner is not sex but another form of affection or love—whether it be heartfelt communication; a nonsexual physical connection, such as cuddling; or something else. Sometimes what you genuinely want is sex. Sometimes it is difficult to know what you want. In a healthy relationship of respect, mutuality, and compassion, you can ask for what you want and need in your relationship. When you do this, you are being responsible for taking care of your wants and needs. You broaden the spectrum of what is possible for you to experience and express.

# Between-Sessions Activity

## Recovery Scale: Sexuality

Please take a few moments to mark the degree to which you do each of the following things. You assessed yourself on this scale at the beginning of this module. Please reassess yourself to see where you are now. You will not have to compare your answers with anyone else, nor will you be judged on how well you do. This is not a test, but an opportunity for you to chart your progress in recovery. After you finish this scale, go back and look at the one you completed at the beginning of the module.

| | Not at All | Just a Little | Pretty Much | Very Much |
|---|---|---|---|---|
| 1. I am comfortable with my body. | | | | |
| 2. I can talk to professionals, including my counselor and my doctor, about sexual concerns. | | | | |
| 3. I can speak appropriately with other people about sexual matters. | | | | |
| 4. I can be affectionate with others. | | | | |
| 5. I am comfortable with my sexual identity. | | | | |
| 6. I am comfortable with my gender identity. | | | | |
| 7. I can accept sexual pleasure from my partner. | | | | |
| 8. I consider my partner's sexual needs and preferences. | | | | |
| 9. I can express my sexual desires to my partner. | | | | |
| 10. I am comfortable having sober sex. | | | | |
| 11. I believe that pleasing myself sexually is healthy. | | | | |
| 12. I understand that sexuality is about more than the physical act of sex. | | | | |

# Reflections on Recovery

In the space below, please write any thoughts, feelings, or questions that you might have about what was covered in this session.

# MODULE D

# Spirituality

Addiction (substance use disorder) can be described as a process of looking outside oneself in order to find something to fill an inner void, something that will make one feel whole and complete. Addiction is a disease of isolation, and one cannot recover in isolation. In recovery, change occurs as a result of building healthier relationships. Spirituality is recognizing that each of us is an integral part of a much greater whole. Recovery can reveal a spiritual path toward inner wholeness, congruence, and integrity.

Some people define spirituality as "connection to the universe," "belief in something greater than the self," "discovering life's purpose," and "trust in a higher or deeper part of myself." This module explores different ways to find spirituality and explains how spirituality is different from religion.

One session in this module focuses on power and privilege and how they get in the way of a person's ability to connect to other people and the community. This can help you better understand the concept of power as you build connections with other people and your community.

This module also invites you to begin to create a vision of the person you want to be. Finally, you have the opportunity to celebrate your time in your group and, even if you are using this workbook on your own, the progress you have made while doing the work of this program.

Finally, when you begin to use this workbook after a group session or on your own, take a minute or two to unwind, relax, and focus on where you are now. Just get settled in the way that feels best for you. Allow yourself to notice how you're breathing and then inhale gently and exhale fully. Repeat the breathing exercise two more times. If you experience difficult feelings during the program, try using one of the grounding activities you are learning in the sessions.

# What Is Spirituality?

In this session, you are introduced to the concept of spirituality and the differences between spirituality and religion. Because spirituality is essentially about connection and relationships, these sessions help you to begin to explore your spiritual self and to feel the power of joining together on a path of self-awareness and spiritual awakening. You will begin to understand the vital role that relationships with self and a power greater-than-self play, not just in recovery but in every area of your life.

The goals of this session are

- To discuss the differences between religion and spirituality
- To develop language for describing our spiritual experiences
- To understand the importance of service in a person's journey
- To reinforce the value of being a part of a community

# Five Senses

This is another tool for managing uncomfortable feelings, such as anxiety, fear, and stress. By focusing on your senses in the "here and now," you will be able to detach from any inner distress you may be experiencing. As with all grounding activities, the more you practice this, the more effective it becomes.

1. Close your eyes and relax for about fifteen seconds.
2. Now open your eyes.
3. Silently, identify five things you can see around you.
4. Identify four things you can feel or touch.
5. Identify three things you can hear.
6. Now identify two things you can smell.
7. Finally, identify one thing you can taste right now.

---

### Five Senses Card

5 things    👁

4 things    ✋

3 things    👂

2 things    👃

1 thing    👅

*Healing Trauma*
Stephanie S. Covington, PhD

Source: *Healing Trauma: A Brief Intervention for Women*, by Stephanie S. Covington and Eileen M. Russo, 2016, rev. 2021. Center City, MN: Hazelden.

---

# Yoga Pose #1

Yoga is an ancient practice that integrates the mind and the body. These simple poses can make a big difference in how grounded you feel at any time in your day.

The first poses are a sequence of three: "Mountain," "Forward Fold," and "Flat Back." If you experience any discomfort or anything makes it difficult for you to do any of the yoga poses, you can simply do the Mountain pose, seated or standing, with or without extending your arms.

1. First, make sure that your core is engaged and your hips are tucked under a little bit. To keep your core engaged, simply tighten your stomach muscles, as if you were doing a crunch without moving your torso.
2. Relax your shoulders and roll them back and down. This is the Mountain.

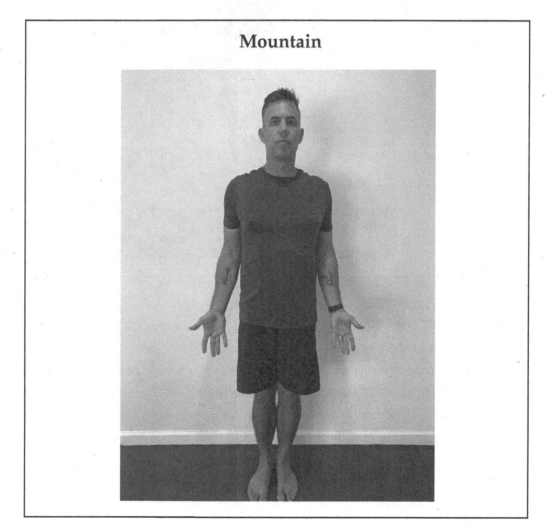

**Mountain**

3. Inhale and raise your arms above your head. This is the Extended
   Mountain pose.

**Extended Mountain**

4. Hold your arms up while exhaling.

5. Inhale and exhale again.

6. Inhale. Now, move your arms out and away from your head while bending
   down from your waist, as if you were diving.

7. Then exhale and bend your knees as much as you need to in order to bend
   down all the way, touching your hands to the floor. This is the Forward Fold.

*Helping Men Recover A Man's Workbook*

## Forward Fold

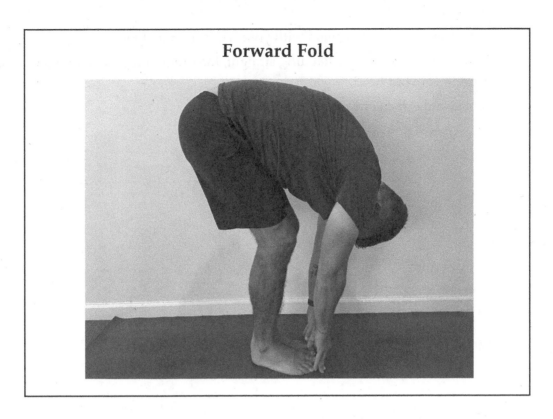

8. Now inhale again and place your hands on your shins while raising your back until it is flat. Keep a small bend in your knees. This is the Flat Back.

## Flat Back

9. Exhale and bend down again with your hands on the floor.

10. Inhale and come back to standing straight, the Mountain pose, with your arms raised over your head.

11. Inhale and exhale one more time.

# Spirituality, Religion, and Addiction

For some people, discomfort with the concept of spirituality is really discomfort with religion as they have observed or experienced it. Some of us have had positive experiences with religion, and others have not. It's possible to be religious without being spiritual, and it's possible to be spiritual without being religious. It is also possible to be both.

Religion has to do with the content of what you believe and the practices by which you express those beliefs. Religion is a system of beliefs, rituals, and values followed by a specific group of people who organize around those beliefs, rituals, and values. When cut off from true spirituality, religion consists of dogma, structures, and rules.

Spirituality is an experience of connection to something greater than yourself in which you engage at a personal and emotional level. In true spirituality, the important thing is your own experience of what is central in the universe: your own relationship with a universal power, whether you call it God, Allah, Buddha, nature, the Great Spirit, a higher power, or something else. In fact, there does not even have to be another "power" involved. Many atheists and agnostics have found recovery and spirituality. An atheist is someone who does not believe in a supreme being. An agnostic is someone who is not sure whether a supreme being exists. One way that you can look at spirituality is moving from living in a self-centered universe to living in a broad and ever-expanding universe in which you are only a small but essential part. In short, there is much more power and satisfaction in "We" than in "I."

Having a relationship with a power that is greater than themselves, that will care for and love them unconditionally, helps many people to change how they experience power in their relationships. Individuals who have suffered from abuse of power may be more comfortable thinking of something deeper or wider, rather than as a higher power to which they must submit. People need to find their own relationships with something meaningful outside themselves that works for them, and this will evolve over time. As you grow in recovery, your sense of spirituality likely will grow as well.

Addiction is as much a spiritual disease as a physical one. Many psychologists conclude that all humans have an inborn desire for a connection to what is most real and meaningful. But our society encourages us to look for satisfaction in things such as achievement, possessions, people's approval, sex, status, and alcohol and other drugs. The desire for something better is a good and normal impulse, but we need to start looking for something that will fill the void in a power that is higher, deeper, and wider than us and any kind of drug.

# Discussion Questions

1. Think back to your childhood. What was the role of religion in your family?

2. Was religion a positive experience for you then or a negative one? In what ways?

3. What religious practices have you engaged in as an adult? Has your drinking or drug use had any effect on your religious practices? If so, how?

4. Have you engaged in any nonreligious spiritual practices either as a child or an adult? What have these been like for you?

5. Do you have any specific ideas or plans to bring more spirituality into your life now that you are engaged in a program of recovery? What are some of these?

# Barriers to the Spiritual Journey

There are certain behaviors and attitudes that promote spirituality, and there are behaviors and attitudes that are barriers to spirituality.

What are some words to describe behaviors and attitudes that are nonspiritual in nature? Some examples are "dishonest," "resentful," "afraid," "closed-minded," "selfish," "prejudiced," and "self-indulgent." What others can you think of?

# Behaviors That Promote the Spiritual Journey

What are some words to describe behaviors and attitudes that are spiritual in nature? Some examples for "spiritual" are "honest," "open," "tolerant," "compassionate," "disciplined," "grateful," "loving," and "understanding." What others can you think of?

# To Be of Service

Many people in recovery have discovered that one of the greatest tools to help them fill the spiritual void is being of service. Being of service means helping other people, organizations, our communities, and other good causes. Each of us already has many of the tools a person needs to be happy. In sobriety, it is simply a matter of using them in the right ways. One of the best ways is to make other people's days or lives a little better.

It is a common stereotype that men are selfish. The irony is that many of us do spend a lot of time trying to get what we think we want at any cost, and it makes us miserable. Yet we keep doing it. There is nothing more self-centered than addiction. When we learn how to be of service to others, we also begin to see the true value of being in recovery.

In the Twelve Step community, being of service to another person is the essence of recovery. When you go to a meeting and reach to shake the hand of someone who is newer than you; or when you make the coffee, sweep the floor, or lead a meeting; or when you call another member of your group to see how that person is doing, that is service. The members of the Twelve Step community have discovered that, when they seek to help others, they stay sober.

You may feel guilty about how selfish you have been and go to the extreme of trying to help everyone. You may feel pressured to say "Yes" any time someone asks you for help. But your ability to be useful to others will depend on your ability to say establish healthy boundaries and say "No" when you need to. You will need to find your own balance.

# Creative Expression Project

This is an opportunity to do a creative project. Using whatever artistic medium you would like, create a project that explores the person you want to be. You can play a musical piece, draw a picture or do some other kind of art project, read spoken words or a poem, create a song or rap, or utilize some other creative format. You will have time to work on your projects and will not be asked to share them until Session 21. As always, you will be invited to share, but doing so is optional.

# Between-Sessions Activities

1. Please complete this Recovery Scale on spirituality. As before, you will complete the scale now and then again at the end of this module.

2. Please also begin planning your creative expression project.

## Recovery Scale: Spirituality

Please take a few moments to mark the degree to which each of the following things is true for you. Make an "X" or a circle on each line to indicate your response. You will not have to compare your answers with anyone else's, and you will not be judged on how well you are doing. This is not a test, but an opportunity for you to chart your own progress in recovery.

| | Not at All | Just a Little | Pretty Much | Very Much |
|---|---|---|---|---|
| 1. I acknowledge my spiritual needs. | | | | |
| 2. I understand the difference between religion and spirituality. | | | | |
| 3. I find comfort in my spiritual practices. | | | | |
| 4. I have a deep relationship and connection with God/Allah/a higher power. | | | | |
| 5. I feel connected to others. | | | | |
| 6. I respect the spiritual beliefs and practices of others. | | | | |
| 7. I practice some form of daily prayer or meditation. | | | | |
| 8. I am aware of my feelings of grief and loss. | | | | |
| 9. I trust my inner wisdom. | | | | |
| 10. I have a vision for my life. | | | | |
| 11. I live one day at a time. | | | | |
| 12. I am grateful for the life I have today. | | | | |

# Reflections on Recovery

In the space below, please write any thoughts, feelings, or questions that you might have about what was covered in this session.

# Power and Privilege

In this session, you examine the concepts of power and privilege. In our society, as in many, people raised as men (especially white heterosexual men) often see themselves as having higher status and being deserving of special treatment. Often, this attitude and its benefits are taken for granted. However, some of the behaviors associated with this assumption are harmful to women and children. Both men and women are constricted by the traditional roles imposed on them by society. Women often are limited in what they are allowed to do and can aspire to. Men are limited in how they relate to others, what they experience emotionally, and where they are supposed to dedicate their energies. Understanding power and privilege is spiritual work because it gives you an opportunity to live in your family and community with greater connection and empathy.

Although men are part of a dominant group, some also belong to marginalized groups, such as being non-white or being gay or trans, which complicates the dynamics of power and privilege.

This session also introduces the practice of meditation. Practices such as prayer and meditation are important to the spiritual life in the same way that practicing a musical instrument is important to making music. Meditation offers a chance to discover the values of solitude and stillness.

*A Man's Workbook: Helping Men Recover, A Program for Treating Addiction*, Second Edition.
Stephanie S. Covington, Dan Griffin, and Rick Dauer.
© 2022 Stephanie S. Covington, Dan Griffin, and Rick Dauer. Published 2022 by John Wiley & Sons, Inc.

The goals of this session are

- To explore how power influences our relationships and how we connect with others
- To examine the costs of privilege and how it influences lives in ways that we never imagined
- To understand how meditation can help to enhance spirituality

# Yoga Pose #2

These poses are "Seated Cat" and "Cow." You can do them on the floor if you feel more comfortable that way. Remember, if you are experiencing any discomfort or are unable to do these exercises, you can do the Mountain pose that was presented in the last session, while seated or standing.

If you choose the floor option, place your hands on the floor directly under your shoulders and place your knees on the floor in line with your hips, while keeping your back in a flat, neutral position, which is called the "Table Top."

## In a Chair

1. Sit up in your chair. Then slide forward a little bit. Place your hands on your knees. This is the "Seated Neutral" position.

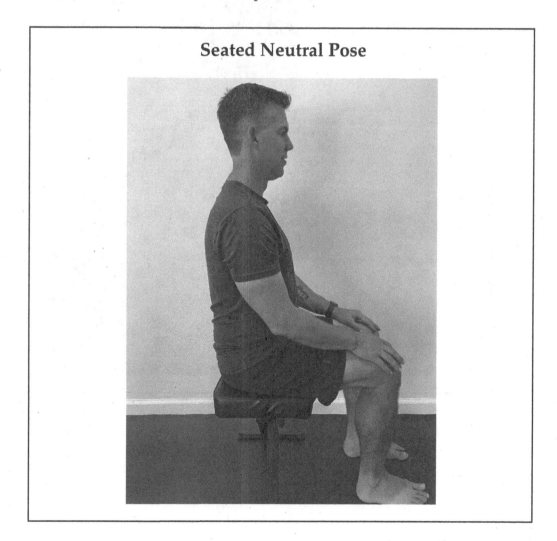

**Seated Neutral Pose**

2. Now take a deep breath in and let it out. As you breathe in again, gently arch your back while pressing your chest forward and lifting your chin. This is called "Seated Cow."

**Seated Cow**

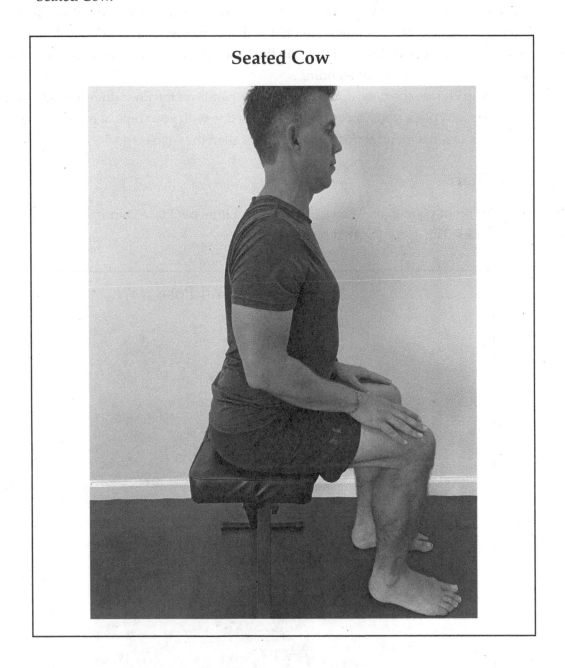

*Helping Men Recover A Man's Workbook*

3. As you breathe out, round your back and drop your chin to your chest while pulling your belly back toward you. This is called "Seated Cat."

**Seated Cat**

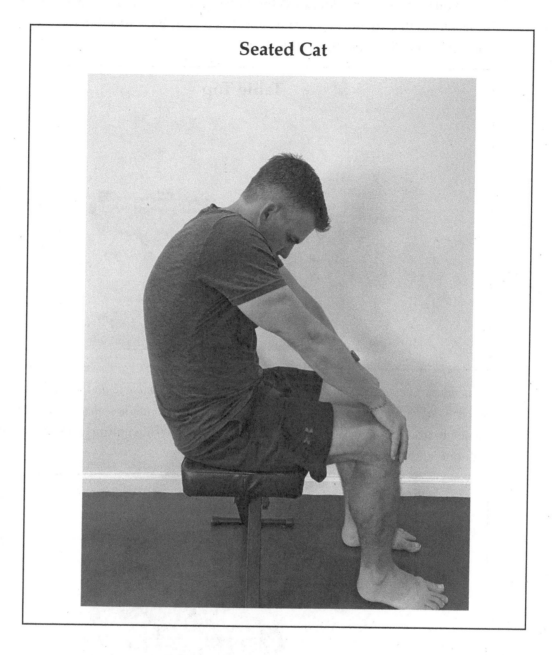

4. Now repeat the positions.
   - Breathe in, Cow.
   - Breathe out, Cat.

## On the Floor

1. Place your hands on the floor directly under your shoulders and place your knees on the floor in line with your hips. Keep your back in a flat, neutral position, which is called the "Table Top."

**Table Top**

*Remember, if you are experiencing any discomfort or are unable to do these exercises, you can do the Mountain pose that we learned last session, while seated or standing.*

2. Now breathe in, arch your back, and lift your chin while getting long from your tailbone to the top of your head. This is the Cow.

**Cow**

*Helping Men Recover A Man's Workbook*

3. Then, while breathing out, tuck your chin to your chest, round your shoulders, and round your back while lifting your belly in tight. This is the Cat.

**Cat**

4. Now return to the neutral position and just focus on your breath.

# Power

Our dominant culture runs according to a system that is based on power, in which some people hold dominant roles while others hold subordinate roles. Many men have more power and privilege simply because they are men. Here are two lists: a list of people in dominant or powerful roles and a list of people in subordinate or less powerful roles.

| The Power Chart | |
|---|---|
| **Holds Power** | **Receives Oppression** |
| Men | Women, feminine-presenting people, gender nonconforming people |
| White people | People of color, indigenous and multiracial people, and other minorities |
| Owning class, managerial class (wealthy) | Poor, working class |
| Adults | Young people |
| Adults | Elders/seniors |
| Heterosexuals | Queers/lesbians/gays/bisexuals |
| Cisgender people (cis men and cis women)* | Trans people and gender nonconforming people |
| Native English speakers | People whose first language is other than English |
| U.S. citizens | Refugees/immigrants |
| People from developed nations or the "Global North" | People from nondeveloped nations or the "Global South" |
| Christians | Muslims, Jews, atheists, and others |
| Bosses | Workers |
| Teachers | Students |
| College-educated | Not college-educated |
| Labeled "normal"/ neurotypical | Neurodivergent or having a mental/psychiatric/developmental disorder |
| Labeled "normal" body size | Labeled "fat" |
| Enabled | Living with a physical, emotional, mental, or learning disability, whether visible or hidden |

*Gender identity matches the sex assigned at birth*

Source: Adapted with permission from *Helping Teens Stop Violence, Build Community and Stand for Justice* by Allan Creighton and Paul Kivel. Available at https://paulkivel.com/resource/the-power-chart-tool/

*Helping Men Recover A Man's Workbook*

If you are a person described in the left column, you may be unaware of how much power and privilege you have. But if you are a person described in the right column, you probably have a pretty good idea of how much power you do not have. Powerful people generally have better police protection and are given more respect at work and in social situations. Disadvantaged people may be subject to stereotyping, discrimination, harassment, and exploitation.

*Privilege* is defined as "unearned and undeserved rights or advantages, obtained simply by membership in a particular group or identity." There are different forms of privilege. Each group that has power over another group usually can be said to have some form of privilege. Adult males, as a group, often are given benefits and advantages over females and children simply because they are male. There is also white privilege, which comes as a result of white people traditionally being in charge of systems of governmental, financial, law enforcement, and social institutions; and the limited opportunities of non-white people.

A *stigma* is a characteristic that society interprets negatively—for example: the stigma of homelessness, the stigma of being overweight, the stigma of mental illness, the stigma of substance misuse, and the stigma of being incarcerated. One's race, class, sexual orientation, gender expression, legal status, physical condition, relationship status, age, size, or appearance can carry a stigma. Such labeling can influence a person's sense of self.

If you are a person in a less powerful group, you probably know quite a bit about how people in the powerful group think. But dominant people tend not to know so much about what it's like to be in a subordinate role. For instance, women tend to know a lot more about men than men know about women. Blacks, Latinx, and Asian Americans know a lot more about whites than whites know about them. Lesbians, gay men, and transgender people know a lot more about straight people than straight people know about them. The reason for this is that dominants often don't value subordinates and often believe that subordinates have nothing to teach them, whereas subordinates learn as much as possible about the dominant culture in order to survive in it.

There also is a myth that dominant people will protect subordinates. Men are supposed to take care of women, the rich are supposed to take care of the poor, and adults are supposed to take care of children. In reality, dominant people frequently abuse subordinates. Some of them believe that dominant people are more valuable than subordinate people, so it's okay for them to use and abuse subordinates. Think about how that may have been true in your experience as a gay man, a child, a person of color, a worker, a prisoner, or in another subordinate role. Or maybe you have been the man, the adult, the white person, or the rich person who could take advantage of someone with less power.

The challenge for men is understanding the power they do have, simply for being men, when they may not have power in other areas of their lives. What is important is to understand that society tends to give members of a privileged group more power, more attention, and more resources.

Step One of the Twelve Steps says, "We admitted we were powerless over alcohol." This applies to other drugs as well. You may struggle with that step because you have felt powerless in other areas of your life. Because men are raised to worship power, the idea of powerlessness could be foreign and scary. Yet Step One asks us to admit our powerlessness over our addictions, not over everything. By admitting our powerlessness over our addictions, we free ourselves to turn our attention to areas in which we do have control and power. We have the power to make better choices in the future than we have made in the past. We do have the power to say what we feel and what we want.

# Power, Privilege, and Behavior

Despite the many social changes that have occurred over the last half century, the most common arena in which power and control are contested is in an intimate relationship. Many men are still socialized to believe that they should be the heads of their households and the primary financial providers. They believe that they should make the important decisions and be the sexual initiators, and that failure to fulfill these roles diminishes their masculinity. Although many men verbalize a more enlightened view of gender relations, these old beliefs continue to influence the ways in which they regard themselves and others, and this is especially true when they are triggered or stressed. In a fight or flight situation, you may find yourself fighting for control and acting out in ways that you would never consider when you were calm and more grounded.

These are behaviors that are examples of male privilege:

1. If you are straight, you are not likely to be abused by your partner or be told to continue living in an abusive household because of your children.
2. As a child, you were able to find plenty of non-limiting images of men in the media.
3. Colloquial phrases and conventional language reflect your gender's dominance (e.g., the word "men" to describe the human race, "mailman," "all men are created equal").
4. Every major religion in the world is led by individuals of your gender.
5. You can have promiscuous sex and be viewed positively for it.
6. A majority of men expect to be taken care of at home and at work (e.g., meals prepared, laundry done, coffee made).
7. You can expect to be paid equitably for the work you do, not paid less because of your gender.
8. You can be confident that your coworkers won't assume you were hired because of your gender.
9. If you are straight, you can walk alone at night without the fear of being sexually assaulted.

# Discussion Questions (Round 1)

1. How do you feel after hearing this list?

2. What do you think it is like for a woman hearing this list?

# Discussion Questions (Round 2)

1. How has your experience as a member of a dominant group affected your behavior?

2. How has your experience as a member of a subordinate group affected your behavior?

3. What pain have you caused others as a member of a dominant group?

4. What pain have you experienced as a member of a subordinate group?

# True Identity

Think back to the Power Chart. For each of the following categories (identities) please indicate whether you see yourself as being in the dominant or subordinate group. Circle which level of status most applies to you.

| Age | Dominant | Subordinate |
|---|---|---|
| | | |
| Gender | Dominant | Subordinate |
| | | |
| Cultural Background | Dominant | Subordinate |
| | | |
| Sexuality | Dominant | Subordinate |
| | | |
| Religion | Dominant | Subordinate |
| | | |
| Physical Ability/Disability | Dominant | Subordinate |
| | | |
| Education | Dominant | Subordinate |
| | | |
| Socioeconomic Class | Dominant | Subordinate |

Respond to the following questions, writing your answers in the space provided.

1. Which identity is the most important or meaningful to you at this point in your life?

2. Which identity causes you to feel pride?

*Helping Men Recover A Man's Workbook*

3. Which identity do you tend to downplay or keep hidden?

4. Which identity do other people tend to judge you by?

5. Which identity gives you advantage over others (privilege)?

6. Which identity puts you at a disadvantage with others (lack of privilege)?

7. Which identity do you know the least about?

8. Which identity would you like to learn more about?

# Breathing Meditation

Meditation offers us the opportunity to use silence to quiet our minds and to increase our self-awareness.

1. Put your feet on the floor, empty your hands and lap, sit up straight, and close your eyes. If you prefer not to close your eyes, you may lower your eyelids.

2. Focus on your breath as it comes out of your nose. This is just like the breathing exercises you have been doing so far in this program. These breathing exercises have been preparing you to learn how to meditate. Your only task is to focus on your breath.

3. Do this breathing for four minutes.

4. Keep breathing and follow your breath as it flows in and out of your nose.

5. If feelings come up, try to mentally stand back and observe them, then let them go. Don't let the fact that you can't stop thinking have you believe that you aren't meditating "correctly." Just return to your breath.

6. Just keep bringing your attention back to your breathing. Breathe slowly in and slowly out again.

7. If you find your mind wandering, try not to get upset with yourself. This is normal. Just bring your mind gently back to your breathing.

8. Do this for three or four more minutes.

9. Bring your attention back to the room. Feel your feet on the floor, feel your back in your chair. When you are ready, open your eyes.

# Between-Sessions Activity

Between now and the next session, your task is to continue working on your creative expression project. Using whatever artistic medium you would like, create a project that explores the person you want to be. Like the letters you did earlier, you can do an art project, a spoken word or poem, or a song, or you can use any creative format that works best for you. You will not be asked to share your project until Session 21, which is two sessions from now. As always, sharing is optional.

# Reflections on Recovery

In the space below, please write any thoughts, feelings, or questions that you might have about what was covered in this session.

# Building Resilience

In this session you explore the intersection of addiction, trauma, and spirituality. Addiction and trauma have profound impacts on a person's life. There is a hole that grows inside as the person's addiction grows. That hole is compounded by the experience of trauma and the wounds that the person carries, often unknowingly. Spirituality offers a way for people to make sense of some of their suffering.

In this session, you also consider grief and loss—topics that most addicted people struggle with. And you learn about resilience: how people can become more capable in bouncing back from adverse experiences.

Finally, you will have the opportunity to think once again about The Man Rules and exactly what kind of man you want to be in recovery.

The goals of this session are

- To understand the value of exploring grief and loss
- To recognize the wisdom and strength we gain through our struggles
- To create one's own definition of masculinity

*A Man's Workbook: Helping Men Recover, A Program for Treating Addiction,* Second Edition.
Stephanie S. Covington, Dan Griffin, and Rick Dauer.
© 2022 Stephanie S. Covington, Dan Griffin, and Rick Dauer. Published 2022 by John Wiley & Sons, Inc.

# Yoga Pose #3

The third yoga pose is called the "Plank." This can be done using a chair or on the floor.

## In a Chair

1. Sitting upright in a chair, adopt the neutral pose.

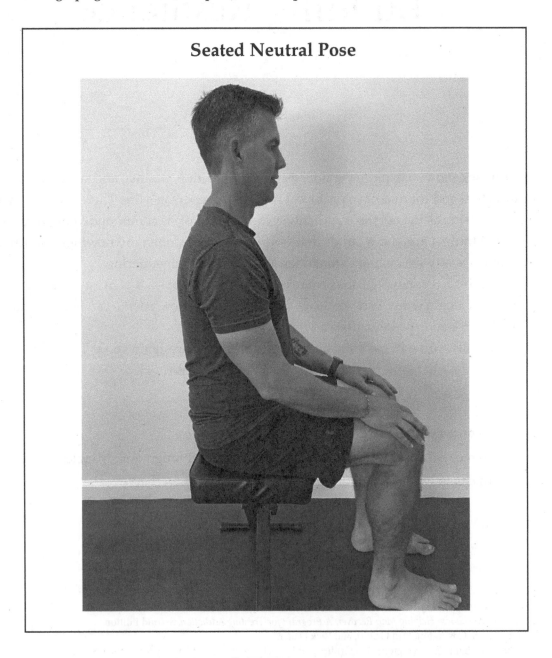

**Seated Neutral Pose**

*Helping Men Recover A Man's Workbook*

2. Stand up straight and face your chair. Place both hands on top of or gripping the sides of the chair.

3. Lean forward, with your arms supporting the weight of your body.

4. Try to keep your head, your neck, your torso, and your legs all at the same angle to the chair. Make sure that your body is straight and your back is flat.

**Chair Plank**

5. Breathe in and breathe out while holding the pose. Focus on your breath.

6. Hold the pose for about thirty seconds. Do not injure yourself doing it if you feel any pain.

## On the Floor

1. To do these poses on the floor, get on your hands and knees on the floor.

2. Now get into what is called the Table Top or neutral position.

## Table Top

3. Now, so long as you are not injured or having any back pain, keep your hands planted on the ground while raising your knees off the ground and straightening your legs.

   If you have any back or leg pain, you can keep your knees on the ground and simply lean forward while keeping your hands on the ground.

## Plank

4. Breathe in and breathe out while holding the pose.
5. Hold the pose for about thirty seconds. Do not injure yourself doing it if you feel any pain. It is harder than it looks!

Thank you for trying out this pose. It may have been harder than you expected.

# Addiction, Trauma, and Spirituality

Trauma can haunt us. Often, we allow our pain to disconnect us from ourselves, from others, and from any sense of a higher power or something bigger than ourselves. We do not even know that it is happening. Our pain leads us to addiction, which separates us even more. For those who struggle with addiction and past trauma, it is hard to feel connected. It is hard to feel as if there is a purpose to life. We tell ourselves that we are alone and that nobody will understand. We keep secrets from others and even from ourselves.

Addiction is a lonely and self-destructive journey. When people are active in their addictions, it is like they are trying to outrun something. They use, and they find that the hole inside just keeps getting bigger. If we do not heal the effects of trauma, we can be in danger of relapse.

Spirituality frees us. The spiritual part of recovery helps us to reconnect to the world. Spirituality offers us the opportunity to heal the parts of us that we think are broken—the parts that perhaps others have told us are broken. When we begin to heal, we realize that we are offered something so much bigger than just the easing of our pain. It's a whole new world in which we can live.

One of the worst parts of the trauma is feeling like a victim. Having spirituality in your life offers you the opportunity to let that go. This doesn't mean that you were not victimized at one point of your life, because you may have been. But there has never been freedom or peace for anyone who is unwilling to let go of the identity of being a victim.

We do not have to let our traumatic experiences be the central players in our stories. Spirituality can give us access to a new perspective that can help us write new stories.

# Grief

When we are walking a spiritual path, we are more aware of our feelings and emotional responses. It can be difficult to be in touch with our feelings, especially those of grief and loss. One misconception about grieving is that it is about crying. This is not true. Grieving allows us to touch the deepest parts of our humanity and connect to our spirituality. When we grieve, we surrender to the reality that we are not in control of the universe—that things sometimes are completely out of our control.

Some common losses people experience in their recovery are

- The loss of the relationship with your addiction
- The relationships that were unrealized or lost as a result of your addiction
- The loss of regular contact with friends and family members
- The loved ones and friends who have died
- The loss of hopes and aspirations
- The missed opportunities and the regrets that resulted from your addiction
- The loss of your ability to feel
- The loss of your relationship to your higher power
- The loss of your physical health
- The loss of your freedom
- The harm you have caused others, especially those whom you care about or whom you have significantly damaged

The expression of grief is the first stage in the process of healing from loss. Honor the grief inside you and to find a safe place where you can share it and let it go. Having unexpressed grief is like wearing lead boots: You can move around but you are not free. When you keep your grief inside you, it blocks you from realizing the spiritual dimension of life. Your ability to get in touch with your grief and give yourself permission to experience your grief without shame is a critical step in your recovery and your search for spirituality.

# Discussion Questions

1. On a scale of one to ten, with one representing no significant losses, what number would you assign to reflect the losses you have experienced in your life? Please explain.

2. How did you deal with the most recent loss you experienced?

3. Dealing with loss can be difficult. What are ways that you can be easy on yourself while you deal with loss?

4. What are some of the fears that you have about dealing with grief and loss?

5. What would you need to feel safe enough to fully express your feelings of grief and loss?

# Resilience

Psychologists define resilience as the quality of adapting well in the face of adversity, trauma, tragedy, threats, or significant sources of stress, such as family and relationship problems, serious health problems, and workplace and financial stressors.

Resilience is like a muscle that can be strengthened through training and exercise. Here are fifteen things you can do that will increase your ability to be resilient:

1. Establish realistic goals
2. Find a sense of purpose
3. Be optimistic and believe in yourself
4. Focus on past success you have had in facing difficult challenges
5. Achieve balance in your life
6. Develop connections with others
7. Be willing to reach out and ask for support
8. Be willing to step outside your comfort zone and try new things
9. Act according to a set of morals and values
10. Develop a relationship with a power greater than yourself
11. Be aware of high levels of stress and engage in practices to diminish these
12. Reconsider the need to change so that it is seen as opportunity
13. Do not personalize difficulties you may encounter
14. Practice meditation and other spiritual practices
15. Accept that change is a fundamental aspect of being human

Please answer these questions in the spaces that follow.

1. Identify one thing you've done in the past when faced with adversity.

2. Identify one thing you haven't done in the past when faced with adversity, but are capable of and willing to do now.

3. Identify one thing that you would like to learn how to do in the future when faced with adversity.

# A New Definition of Masculinity

People who have been in recovery for some time describe the process as "growing up." They also say that their success in growing up is dictated more by expressing who they really are and living according to the principles of recovery than by any of their old concepts of how to act or how to be.

You have a chance to create a new definition of being a man—one that represents the person you really want to be. Some of the old rules just need some adjustment. Power and control are not bad things; it's how and when we use them that make the difference. Having personal power—control over our behavior and a sense of purpose—is a good thing. Being strong when strength is required is a good thing. Being independent and not going along with the crowd may be a very good thing.

Developing a new definition of masculinity requires self-examination. Consider your past, your present, and your desired future. Learn to accept where you came from and what you've learned along the way. Be honest about who you are and what you really feel. Consider your old behaviors and attitudes and ask which of these have worked for you and which haven't.

# Discussion Questions

1. How do you want to define what it means to be the person you would like to be?

2. Which of The Man Rules that were identified in Session 3 do you believe will continue to work for you and would you like to hold on to? Briefly explain why.

3. What are some of the new rules you would like to add to this list? Explain why.

Becoming the man that you want to be is a physical, emotional, psychological, and spiritual journey. With each step along this journey, it is important to give yourself credit for the distance that you have already traveled.

# Between-Sessions Activity

Between now and the next session, please complete your creative expression project. Be sure to bring your project with you to the next session and be prepared to share it with the group. If you choose not to share, please bring your project anyway. Remember, your efforts to express yourself are what's important. No one will judge your work or compare it to others'.

# Reflections on Recovery

In the space below, please write any thoughts, feelings, or questions that you might have about what was covered in this session.

# Creating a Vision

In this final session, you have an opportunity to articulate your vision of the person you want to be. You are introduced to the idea of living a life with purpose, and you are asked to reflect on the work that you have done in this program. It is hoped that you will feel comfortable verbalizing your deepest desires and purposes and gain a sense of why you are being offered the gift of recovery.

The goals of this session are

- To create a vision of where you want to be six months from now
- To acknowledge the value of the group's time together
- To celebrate the journey the group has taken together

*A Man's Workbook: Helping Men Recover, A Program for Treating Addiction,* Second Edition.
Stephanie S. Covington, Dan Griffin, and Rick Dauer.
© 2022 Stephanie S. Covington, Dan Griffin, and Rick Dauer. Published 2022 by John Wiley & Sons, Inc.

# Your New Definition of Masculinity

In the last session you worked on a new definition of masculinity. What have you learned about yourself in doing it? What challenges or barriers did you face in creating this new definition?

# Share Creative Expression Project

If you are using this workbook individually, you may want to share your Creative Expression Project with your counselor or other advisor (if you have access to one) or with someone who supports your recovery whom you can trust.

# The Ritual of Returning to the Community

Unfortunately, there is a loss of connection in our modern society. Individuals try to survive and "get ahead," and many feel as if they are doing it on their own. Even in their own homes, many people feel isolated. We all need some type of community in which we can feel a sense of belonging and acceptance. Rituals help us to experience our community and our spirituality concretely.

Please identify something in your life that you have been doing by yourself, without help, and then say, ". . . and I am tired of doing it alone." Here is an example: "I have been trying to be a father without any help from anyone and I am tired of doing it alone."

At first, you may feel uncomfortable participating in a ritual like this. Please try to put aside any skepticism and allow yourself to be part of this experience.

Use the space below to make any notes about this. How did it feel?

# Promises of Recovery

The "Big Book" of Alcoholics Anonymous discusses what people in recovery can expect to experience.

---

If we are painstaking about this phase of our development, we will be amazed before we are halfway through. We are going to know a new freedom and a new happiness. We will not regret the past nor wish to shut the door on it. We will comprehend the word serenity and we will know peace. No matter how far down the scale we have gone we will see how our experience can benefit others. That feeling of uselessness and self-pity will disappear. We will lose interest in selfish things and gain interest in our fellows. Self-seeking will slip away. Our whole attitude and outlook upon life will change. Fear of people and of economic insecurity will leave us. We will intuitively know how to handle situations which used to baffle us. We will suddenly realize that God is doing for us what we could not do for ourselves.

Are these extravagant promises? We think not. They are being fulfilled among us—sometimes quickly, sometimes slowly. They will always materialize if we work for them.

This excerpt from *Alcoholics Anonymous*, the Big Book, pages 83–84, is reprinted with permission of Alcoholics Anonymous World Services, Inc. ("A.A.W.S."). Permission to reprint this excerpt does not mean that A.A.W.S. has reviewed or approved the contents of this publication or that A.A. necessarily agrees with the views expressed herein. A.A. is a program of recovery from alcoholism only—use of the Twelve Steps in connection with programs and activities which are patterned after A.A., but which address other problems, or in any other non-A.A. context, does not imply otherwise.

---

You already may be seeing what people call the "promises of recovery" coming true in your life. Remember the way the statement ends: "They will always materialize if we work for them." You have to do the work. The statement does not guarantee you fame and fortune or promise a life that is free of pain. What it promises is that you will learn how to be happy, in the moment, and live comfortably in your skin. It may not happen right away, but the best things in life often happen on a timetable that is much different than it would be if we were in control. The promises are about faith. Trust that they will happen, and they will happen to you as much as they will happen to anyone.

# Gratitude List

A gratitude list is a practice that you can come back to over and over again. There is a saying that no addict has ever relapsed when they were grateful.

Try to fill in all ten spaces by listing what you are grateful for. It does not have to be complicated.

1.

2.

3.

4.

5.

6.

7.

8.

9.

10.

# Prospective Journey

Finding your life's purpose is an essential part of your recovery. Using silence, meditation, and prayer may help you to find it.

In the first blank space, write what the date will be six months from today.

The rest of the page has space for you to write in. Imagine yourself six months from now, writing about where you are on that day and what this six-month journey has been like for you. Write in the present tense, as though you are already at that point in time. If you prefer not to write, you can draw pictures to show your journey and your life at that point.

The date is now_____, and as I look back over the past six months, I see

# Honoring Our Time Together

1. What I have learned about being a man is

2. One thing I will remember most about this experience is

3. One way I am going to make a difference in the larger community is by

4. One way in which I will prioritize my recovery is

# Final Recovery Scale

Please complete this final Recovery Scale in the next day or two. Compare your answers to the scale you completed at the beginning of this module. This will help you to track the changes in your life.

## Recovery Scale: Spirituality

Please take a few moments to mark the degree to which each of the following things is true for you. Make an "X" or a circle on each line to indicate your response. You will not have to compare your answers with anyone else's, and you will not be judged on how well you are doing. This is not a test, but an opportunity for you to chart your own progress in recovery.

| | Not at All | Just a Little | Pretty Much | Very Much |
|---|---|---|---|---|
| 1. I acknowledge my spiritual needs. | | | | |
| 2. I understand the difference between religion and spirituality. | | | | |
| 3. I find comfort in my spiritual practices. | | | | |
| 4. I have a deep relationship and connection with a God/Allah/a higher power. | | | | |
| 5. I feel connected to others. | | | | |
| 6. I respect the spiritual beliefs and practices of others. | | | | |
| 7. I practice some form of daily prayer or meditation. | | | | |
| 8. I am aware of my feelings of grief and loss. | | | | |
| 9. I trust my inner wisdom. | | | | |
| 10. I have a vision for my life. | | | | |
| 11. I live one day at a time. | | | | |
| 12. I am grateful for the life I have today. | | | | |

# Reflections on Recovery

Look back at the "promises" from the Big Book of Alcoholics Anonymous. These promises are for you. You have come a long way in your journey of recovery already, but your new life is just beginning. Take a few minutes answering the questions that follow to reflect on what you have experienced since you began this program. Congratulations on your effort and your work, and best wishes to you.

1. What are some of the things you remember doing?

2. What are some of the things you remember seeing?

3. What are some of the things you remember hearing?

4. What are some of the things you felt during the sessions?

5. What were the high points of the program for you?

6. What were the most difficult points?

7. What was the most valuable thing you gained from being in this program?

There is also a Feedback Form on page 261. Thank you for letting us know about your experience with *Helping Men Recover*.

# Congratulations and Thank You

Congratulations on the work you have done in this program and thank you for your participation. This is the end of the *Helping Men Recover* program, but you can always carry this experience with you as you make new beginnings and decisions about the next steps in your life.

With each ending, space is created for a new beginning. You have started on the new upward path of the spiral. We wish you a great new beginning on your healing journey!

# Additional
# Recovery Resources

# The Twelve Steps of Alcoholics Anonymous

Alcoholics Anonymous was founded in 1935 when two alcoholics joined together to share experiences, strengths, and hopes and found that this sharing enabled them to become and remain sober. They developed the A.A. program around the following Twelve Steps of recovery.

1. We admitted we were powerless over alcohol—that our lives had become unmanageable.
2. Came to believe that a Power greater than ourselves could restore us to sanity.
3. Made a decision to turn our will and our lives over to the care of God *as we understood Him*.
4. Made a searching and fearless moral inventory of ourselves.
5. Admitted to God, to ourselves, and to another human being the exact nature of our wrongs.
6. Were entirely ready to have God remove all these defects of character.
7. Humbly asked Him to remove our shortcomings.
8. Made a list of all persons we had harmed, and became willing to make amends to them all.

*A Man's Workbook: Helping Men Recover, A Program for Treating Addiction*, Second Edition.
Stephanie S. Covington, Dan Griffin, and Rick Dauer.
© 2022 Stephanie S. Covington, Dan Griffin, and Rick Dauer. Published 2022 by John Wiley & Sons, Inc.

9. Made direct amends to such people wherever possible, except when to do so would injure them or others.

10. Continued to take personal inventory and when we were wrong promptly admitted it.

11. Sought through prayer and meditation to improve our conscious contact with God *as we understood Him*, praying only for knowledge of His will for us and the power to carry that out.

12. Having had a spiritual awakening as the result of these steps, we tried to carry this message to alcoholics, and to practice these principles in all our affairs.

The excerpt from *Alcoholics Anonymous*, the Twelve Steps of Alcoholics Anonymous, is reprinted with permission of Alcoholics Anonymous World Services, Inc. ("A.A.W.S."). Permission to reprint this excerpt does not mean that A.A.W.S. has reviewed or approved the contents of this publication, or that A.A. necessarily agrees with the views expressed herein. A.A. is a program of recovery from alcoholism only—use of the Twelve Steps in connection with programs and activities which are patterned after A.A., but which address other problems, or in any other non-A.A. context, does not imply otherwise.

# Recovery Programs

## Alcoholics Anonymous

Alcoholics Anonymous is an international fellowship of people who have or have had a drinking problem. It is nonprofessional, self-supporting, multiracial, apolitical, and available almost everywhere. There are no dues or fees and no age or education requirements.

Alcoholics Anonymous World Services, Inc.
475 Riverside Drive
#1100
New York, NY 10115
Telephone: 800-839-1686
Website: https://www.aa.org

## Cocaine Anonymous

Cocaine Anonymous is a fellowship of people who share their experience, strength, and hope with one another that they may solve their common problem and help others recover from their addiction. The members of C.A. are all recovering addicts who maintain their individual sobriety by working with others. Members come from various social, ethnic, economic, and religious backgrounds, but are not allied with

*A Man's Workbook: Helping Men Recover, A Program for Treating Addiction*, Second Edition.
Stephanie S. Covington, Dan Griffin, and Rick Dauer.
© 2022 Stephanie S. Covington, Dan Griffin, and Rick Dauer. Published 2022 by John Wiley & Sons, Inc.

any sect, denomination, politics, organization, or institution. The only requirement for membership is a desire to stop using cocaine and all other mind-altering substances. There are no dues or fees for membership; C.A. is fully self-supporting through its own contributions.

Cocaine Anonymous World Services, Inc.
P.O. Box 492000
Los Angeles, CA 90049-8000
Telephone: 310-559-5833
Website: www.ca.org

## Narcotics Anonymous

Narcotics Anonymous is a global, community-based organization with a multi-lingual and multicultural membership. It offers recovery from the effects of addiction through working a Twelve Step program, including regular attendance at group meetings. The group atmosphere provides help from peers and offers an ongoing support network for addicts who wish to pursue and maintain a drug-free lifestyle. N.A.'s approach makes no distinction between drugs, including alcohol. Membership is free, and N.A. has no affiliation with any organizations, including governments, religions, law enforcement groups, or medical and psychiatric associations.

NA World Services
P.O. Box 9999
Van Nuys, CA 91409
Telephone: 818-773-9999
Website: https://na.org
E-mail: fsmail@na.org

## Secular Organizations for Sobriety

Secular Organizations for Sobriety (SOS) is a nonprofit network of autonomous, nonprofessional local groups dedicated solely to helping individuals achieve and maintain sobriety/abstinence from alcohol and drug addiction, food addiction, and more.

Secular Organizations for Sobriety
4548 Eichelberger Street
Saint Louis, MO 63116
Telephone: 314-353-3532 (Leave a message with your name and contact information. SOS will return your call within 48 hours.)
Website: http://www.sossobriety.org
E-mail: info@sossobriety.org

## SMART Recovery

SMART Recovery offers free face-to-face and online mutual help groups. SMART Recovery (Self-Management and Recovery Training) helps people recover from all types of addictive behaviors, including alcohol addiction and abuse, drug addiction and abuse, cocaine addiction, gambling addiction, and addiction to other substances and activities. The SMART Recovery four-point program offers specific tools and techniques for each of the program points:

- Point 1: Enhancing and Maintaining Motivation To Abstain
- Point 2: Coping with Urges
- Point 3: Problem Solving (managing thoughts, feelings, and behaviors)
- Point 4: Lifestyle Balance (balancing momentary and enduring satisfactions)

SMART Recovery®
7304 Mentor Avenue, Suite F
Mentor, OH 44060
Telephone: 440-951-5357
Toll-free phone: 866-951-5357
Website: www.smartrecovery.org
E-mail: information@smartrecovery.org

# APPENDIX 3

# Online Recovery Meetings

1. Virtual Alcoholics Anonymous meetings have been available since the birth of the Internet. Being able to connect with other recovering persons at literally any hour of the day without leaving home is a welcome development for many individuals. Many local A.A. central/intergroup offices and area service structures have added information to their websites about how to join a meeting online. You can find online resources at: http://.aa-intergroup.org

2. Cocaine Anonymous Online Service Area: helpline@ca-online.org

3. You also can find a whole online recovery community, including meetings of all types, at www.intherooms.com.

*A Man's Workbook: Helping Men Recover, A Program for Treating Addiction*, Second Edition.
Stephanie S. Covington, Dan Griffin, and Rick Dauer.
© 2022 Stephanie S. Covington, Dan Griffin, and Rick Dauer. Published 2022 by John Wiley & Sons, Inc.

# APPENDIX 4

# Redefining Gender

**Agender:** Describes a person who identifies as not having a gender, or experiences themselves as gender neutral.

**Androgynous:** A combination of masculine and feminine traits or a nontraditional gender expression.

**Cisgender** (pronounced sis-gender): A person whose gender identity matches the sex the person was assigned at birth. (It is sometimes abbreviated as *cis*.)

**Deadnaming:** This is when a person uses the name a transperson was given at birth instead of their chosen name. Generaly experienced as a form of harm.

**Gender binary:** The idea that gender is strictly an either-or option of male/man/masculine or female/woman/feminine based on the sex assigned at birth, rather than a spectrum of gender identities and expressions.

**Gender conforming:** A person whose gender expression is consistent with the cultural norms expected for that gender. According to these norms, boys and men should be masculine, and girls and women should be feminine. Not all cisgender people are gender conforming, and not all transgender people are gender nonconforming. (For example, a transgender woman may have a very feminine gender expression.)

*A Man's Workbook: Helping Men Recover, A Program for Treating Addiction*, Second Edition.
Stephanie S. Covington, Dan Griffin, and Rick Dauer.
© 2022 Stephanie S. Covington, Dan Griffin, and Rick Dauer. Published 2022 by John Wiley & Sons, Inc.

**Gender dysphoria:** The formal diagnosis in the American Psychiatric Association's *Diagnostic and Statistical Manual of Mental Disorders*, fifth edition (*DSM-5*), used by doctors to show that a person meets the diagnostic criteria to begin medical transition. Some in transgender communities disagree with the use of *gender dysphoria*, because it suggests that being transgender is a mental illness rather than an identity. Because a formal diagnosis is usually required for medical treatment in the United States, it does allow access to medical care for people who wouldn't otherwise be eligible to receive it.

**Gender expression:** A person's outward gender presentation, including but not limited to: pronouns, clothing, hairstyle, makeup, jewelry, vocal inflection, body language, and behavior. Gender expression is usually labeled as masculine, feminine, or nonbinary. It can be congruent with a person's gender identity or not.

**Genderfluid:** This is someone whose gender identity or expression is not fixed and may shift according to both internal cues and external context.

**Gender identity:** The gender with which a person identifies; a person's deep-seated, internal sense of who they are as a gendered being.

**Gender marker:** The label (male, female, or another) that appears on a person's official records, such as a birth certificate and driver's license. The gender marker on a transgender person's documents is the sex assigned at birth unless the person legally changes it. Only some parts of the world allow that change.

**Gender nonconforming:** May describe behavior, expression, or a person whose gender expression is inconsistent with the cultural norms expected for their gender, such as boys or men who are not "masculine enough" or are feminine, girls or women who are not "feminine enough" or are masculine.

May also be used for trans or nonbinary people who hae androgynous or mixed gender expression.

**Intersex:** This is an umbrella term for differences in sex traits or reproductive anatomy. Traits can be visible at birth or appear in puberty or later in life and affect approximately 1.7% of people. An antiquated medical term, hermaphrodite, is outdated and offensive, although some people may personally reclaim it.

**LGBTQIA+:** An acronym used to refer to lesbian, gay, bisexual, transgender, queer or questioning, intersex, and asexual or agender individuals and communities. LGBTQIA+ is not a synonym for *nonheterosexual*, as transgender is not a sexual orientation.

**Medical transition:** A long-term series of medical interventions that use hormone treatments and/or surgeries to change a person's body to be more congruent with the person's gender identity. Medical transition is the approved medical treatment for gender dysphoria.

**Nonbinary:** A range of gender identities and expressions, which rejects the notion that gender is strictly an either-or option of male/man/masculine or female/woman/feminine based on the sex assigned at birth. Words that people use to express their nonbinary gender identities include *agender, enby, bigender, genderqueer, genderfluid,* and *pangender*.

**Pronouns:** Affirming pronouns are the most respectful and accurate pronouns for a person, as defined by that person. It's best to ask which pronouns a person uses. In addition to the familiar *he, she,* and *they,* nongendered pronouns include *zie* and *per*.

**Puberty suppression:** A medical process that pauses the hormone changes that trigger puberty in children. The result is delayed development of secondary sex characteristics: breast growth, testicle enlargement, facial hair, body fat redistribution, and voice changes. Suppression allows more time to make decisions about hormone treatment and can prevent transgender youths' increased discomfort with puberty.

**Queer:** An umbrella term for a range of people, behavior, communitiies, and cultures who are not heterosexual and/or cisgender. Historically a slur, "queer" has been widely reclaimed.

**Same-gender loving:** A label sometimes used by members of the Black community to express an alternative sexual orientation without relying on terms and symbols of European descent. The term emerged in the early 1990s with the intention of offering Black women who love women and Black men who love men a voice. It's a way of identifying and being that resonated with the uniqueness of Black culture. (Sometimes abbreviated as SGL.)

**Sex assigned at birth:** The sex someone is labeled at birth, based on the appearance of the genitals.

**Sexual orientation:** A person's feelings of sexual and/or romantic attraction toward other people. Examples: gay, lesbian, bisexual, pansexual, straight (heterosexual), asexual.

**Social transition:** A transgender person's process of creating a life that is congruent with their gender identity, which can include asking others to use a name, pronouns, and gender that is more congruent with their gender identity. It also may involve changing their gender expression to match their gender identity.

**Transgender:** Sometimes abbreviated as *trans,* this adjective is used to describe a person whose gender identity is incongruent with (or does not "match") the sex they were assigned at birth. *Transgender* now serves as an umbrella term to refer to the full range and diversity of identities within transgender communities because it is the most widely used and recognized term.

**Transgender men and boys:** People who identify as male but were assigned female at birth. Also sometimes referred to as *trans men.*

**Transgender women and girls:** People who identify as female but were assigned male at birth. Also sometimes referred to as *trans women.*

**Transsexual:** This outdated term refers to a transgender person who has had hormone treatment and/or surgeries to change their body to be more aligned with their gender identity. It is still used as an identity label by some, but *transgender* has generally become the term of choice. (You should not use this term for people unless they use it for themselves first.)

**Two Spirit:** A term used by Native and Indigenous peoples to indicate that they embody both a masculine and a feminine spirit. It is sometimes also used to describe Native people of diverse sexual orientations and has nuanced meanings in various Indigenous subcultures.

*Note:* A Gender Bingo game is available to help staff and participants learn and understand the definitions. Available at: www.stephaniecovington.com

---

Source: Adapted from Green and Maurer (2015).

# Emotional Sobriety

*This is the substance of a letter that Bill Wilson, co-founder of Alcoholics Anonymous, wrote many years ago to a close friend who also had troubles with depression. The letter appeared in the "Grapevine" in January, 1953.*

I think that many oldsters who have put our AA "booze cure" to severe but successful tests still find they often lack emotional sobriety. Perhaps they will be the spearhead for the next major development in AA, the development of much more real maturity and balance (which is to say, humility) in our relations with ourselves, with our fellows, and with God.

Those adolescent urges that so many of us have for top approval, perfect security, and perfect romance, urges quite appropriate to age seventeen, prove to be an impossible way of life when we are at age forty-seven and fifty-seven.

Since AA began, I've taken immense wallops in all these areas because of my failure to grow up emotionally and spiritually. My God, how painful it is to keep demanding the impossible, and how very painful to discover, finally, that all along we have had the cart before the horse. Then comes the final agony of seeing how awfully wrong we have been, but still finding ourselves unable to get off the emotional merry-go-round.

How to translate a right mental conviction into a right emotional result, and so into easy, happy and good living. Well, that's not only the neurotic's problem, it's the

*A Man's Workbook: Helping Men Recover, A Program for Treating Addiction*, Second Edition.
Stephanie S. Covington, Dan Griffin, and Rick Dauer.
© 2022 Stephanie S. Covington, Dan Griffin, and Rick Dauer. Published 2022 by John Wiley & Sons, Inc.

problem of life itself for all of us who have got to the point of real willingness to hew to right principles in all of our affairs.

Even then, as we hew away, peace and joy may still elude us. That's the place so many of us AA oldsters have come to. And it's a hell of a spot, literally. How shall our unconscious, from which so many of our fears, compulsions, and phony aspirations still stream, be brought into line with what we actually believe, know, and want! How to convince our dumb, raging and hidden "Mr. Hyde" becomes our main task.

I've recently come to believe that this can be achieved. I believe so because I begin to see many benighted ones, folks like you and me, commencing to get results. Last autumn, depression, having no really rational cause at all, almost took me to the cleaners. I began to be scared that I was in for another long chronic spell. Considering the grief I've had with depressions, it wasn't a bright prospect.

I kept asking myself "Why can't the Twelve Steps work to release depression?" By the hour, I stared at the St. Francis Prayer. . . "It's better to comfort than to be comforted." Here was the formula, all right, but why didn't it work?

Suddenly, I realized what the matter was. My basic flaw had always been dependence, almost absolute dependence, on people or circumstances to supply me with prestige, security, and the like. Failing to get these things according to my perfectionist dreams and specifications, I had fought for them. And when defeat came, so did my depression.

There wasn't a chance of making the outgoing love of St. Francis a workable and joyous way of life until these fatal and almost absolute dependencies were cut away.

Because I had over the years undergone a little spiritual development, the absolute quality of these frightful dependencies had never before been so starkly revealed. Reinforced by what grace I could secure in prayer, I found I had to exert every ounce of will and action to cut off these faulty emotional dependencies upon people, upon AA, indeed upon any act of circumstance whatsoever.

Then only could I be free to love as Francis did. Emotional and instinctual satisfactions, I saw, were really the extra dividends of having love, offering love, and expressing love appropriate to each relation of life.

Plainly, I could not avail myself to God's love until I was able to offer it back to Him by loving others as He would have me. And I couldn't possibly do that so long as I was victimized by false dependencies.

For my dependence meant demand, a demand for the possession and control of the people and the conditions surrounding me.

While those words "absolute dependence" may look like a gimmick, they were the ones that helped to trigger my release into my present degree of stability and quietness of mind, qualities which I am now trying to consolidate by offering love to others regardless of the return to me.

This seems to be the primary healing circuit: an outgoing love of God's creation and His people, by means of which we avail ourselves of His love for us. It is most clear that the real current can't flow until our paralyzing dependencies are broken, and broken at depth. Only then can we possibly have a glimmer of what adult love really is.

If we examine every disturbance we have, great or small, we will find at the root of it some unhealthy dependence and its consequent demand. Let us, with God's help, continually surrender these hobbling demands. Then we can be set free to live and love: we may then be able to gain emotional sobriety.

Of course, I haven't offered you a really new idea—only a gimmick that has started to unhook several of my own hexes at depth. Nowadays, my brain no longer races compulsively in either elation, grandiosity or depression. I have been given a quiet place in bright sunshine.

*Bill Wilson*

The "Emotional Sobriety" (c. 1950) letter by Bill Wilson is reproduced courtesy of the Stepping Stones Foundation Archive at Stepping Stones—Historic Home of Bill & Lois Wilson, Katonah, New York, steppingstones.org. It is from the William Griffith Wilson (WGW) Collection 102—Correspondence, Box 11, Folder 9. Permission is required for further use.

# FEEDBACK FORM

Dear Participant:

I would appreciate hearing about your experience with the *Helping Men Recover* program. Any information or feedback you would like to share with us will be greatly appreciated.

Describe yourself:

_____

_____

Where did you participate in this program?

_____

_____

Describe your experience with the program:

_____

_____

_____

_____

*A Man's Workbook: Helping Men Recover, A Program for Treating Addiction,* Second Edition.
Stephanie S. Covington, Dan Griffin, and Rick Dauer.
© 2022 Stephanie S. Covington, Dan Griffin, and Rick Dauer. Published 2022 by John Wiley & Sons, Inc.

What did you find most useful?

_____

_____

Why? How?

_____

_____

What did you find least useful?

_____

_____

Why? How?

_____

_____

What was missing from the program that you wish had been covered?

_____

_____

Other suggestions/comments:

_____

_____

Thank you for your input.

Please return this survey to:                Contact information for coauthors:
Stephanie S. Covington, PhD, LCSW           Dan Griffin, MA: dan@dangriffin.com
Institute for Relational Development        Rick Dauer, LADC: rickdauer1@gmail.com
Center for Gender & Justice
7946 Ivanhoe Avenue, Suite 201B
La Jolla, CA 92037
Fax: (858) 454-8598
Email: sc@stephaniecovington.com
Website: www.stephaniecovington.com